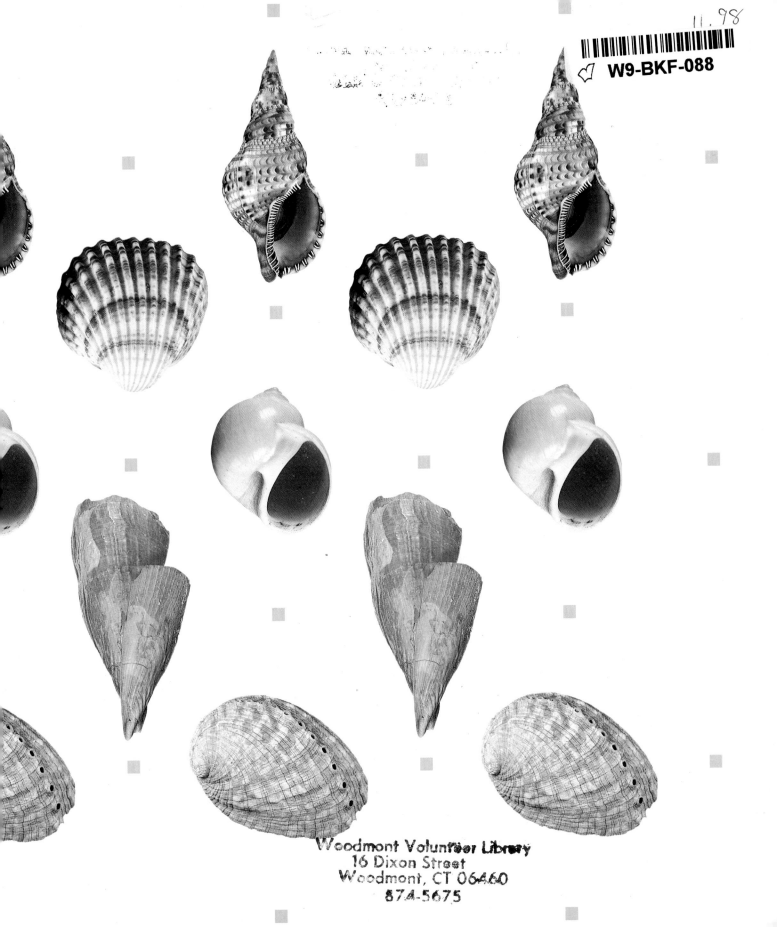

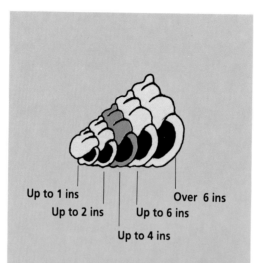

Up to 1 ins

Up to 2 ins

Up to 4 ins

Up to 6 ins

Over 6 ins

Shell Size Scale

This symbol is shown beside each shell. The purple-colored section shows you at a glance how big the shell is likely to be. But the size may vary because the shell goes on growing with its owner. In this example the shell will be between 2 and 4 inches (ins) long.

SCIENCE NATURE GUIDES

SEASHELLS
OF NORTH AMERICA

TUCKER ABBOTT

EDITED BY
Theodore Rowland-Entwistle

THUNDER BAY
P·R·E·S·S

Conservation

Empty shells are no longer wanted by their owners, so you do not need to worry about taking them. However, don't forget that tiny hermit crabs, which have no shells of their own, use large empty shells to hide in. If you find live mollusks in rock pools, study them but do not disturb them, unless you have a special aquarium and plenty of fresh sea-water to go in it (see page 50).

Shell collectors kill far fewer mollusks than do commercial fishermen, birds, crabs, and storms, but it is still better to leave live mollusks in their homes. On page 78, you will find the names of some organizations who campaign for the preservation of sea creatures and the environment. By joining them and supporting their efforts, you can help to preserve our coasts and seas for the future.

Shell Collector's Code

Remember that beaches can be dangerous places as well as pleasant ones.
1 **Keep a careful eye on the tide**, and make sure you can reach safety if the tide starts to come in.
2 **Make sure somebody knows where you are**, so that help can come if you need it, and **always** go with a companion.
3 **Don't walk under overhanging cliffs.**
4 **Avoid doing any damage to the environment**, or harming any living creature you may come across.
4 **Take your litter home with you.**
5 **Ask permission before crossing private property** to reach a beach or going on a private wharf.

Thunder Bay Press
5880 Oberlin Drive, Suite 400
San Diego, CA 92121

First p ublished in the United States
by Thunder Bay Press, 1994
Reprinted 1994

© Dragon's World, 1994
© Text Dragon's World, 1994

Complete Cataloging in Publication (CIP)
is available through the Library of Congress.
LC Card Number: 93–46147

The author and publishers would like to thank
Dr R. Tucker Abbott for loaning the majority of the
photographs illustrating this book.
© R. Tucker Abbott, 1994
© David Parmiter, 1994: pages 8–9, 58–59
Activity illustrations by Richard Coombes;
headbands by Antonia Phillips

Edited text and captions by Theodore Rowland-Entwistle, based on *Seashells of the Northern Hemisphere* by R. Tucker Abbott.

Editor	Diana Briscoe
Designer	James Lawrence
Design Assistant	Victoria Furbisher
Editorial Director	Pippa Rubinstein

Printed in Italy

ISBN 1 85028 264 1

Contents

Introduction

Seashells are all over the Atlantic and Pacific beaches of North America. These hard, colorful cases were once the homes of living animals, relatives of the snails that you find in your yard. They belong to a group called the mollusks.

You can learn a lot about mollusks and their life by collecting their shells and studying live specimens in temporary aquariums. This book will show you how to collect them, and explains the different kinds of mollusks. The shells come from animals living near the shore.

There are over 60,000 different seashells world-wide, but you are unlikely to find more than a few hundred even if you search every beach in the USA! This book shows you the most common shells.

Some mollusks live in warm water, others in colder water. This book divides the seas around North America into four areas, according to the average sea temperature. Some species can be found in more than one area, because they can tolerate a wide range of temperatures or have adapted to local conditions.

Mollusks lay masses of eggs, because only a few will survive

As the mollusk grows, its shell grows with it. When it is fully formed, it will be ready to produce more eggs

The egg hatches into a larva

The larva begins to grow a shell. Its oar-like flaps are covered with tiny hairs, which help it to swim until it finds a rock or other place to settle

Life of a Seashell

Different species of mollusks reproduce themselves in different ways. Some mollusks leave their eggs to float freely in the water. Others hide them in the sand, in a living sponge, or in a fold of their own bodies. Some species of mollusk have separate males and females (as humans do). In other mollusks the same animal is both male and female.

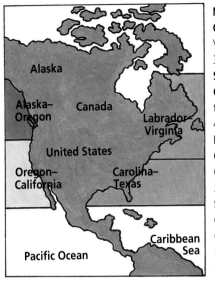

Northern Atlantic Coast: Labrador to Virginia. Water heat is 32° to 52° Fahrenheit.

Southern Atlantic Coast: North Carolina to Texas. Water heat is 45° to 85° Fahrenheit.

Northern Pacific Coast: Alaska to Oregon. Water heat is 32° to 52° Fahrenheit.

Southern Pacific Coast: Oregon to California. Water heat is 45° to 75° Fahrenheit.

How to use this book

To identify a shell you do not recognize—for example the two shown left—follow these steps.

1 **Find the section of this book** that describes your area.

2 **Decide what kind of beach you are on.** Does it have rocky pools or sand or mud flats? Is it an estuary or are you looking at a part of the beach that is covered at high tide? Each habitat (type of beach) has a different picture band (see below).

3 **Decide what sort of mollusk you have found.** Is it a gastropod or a bivalve? See pages 6 and 7 if you don't know the difference.

4 **Look through the pages of shells** of this type and heading. The information and photo given for each

mollusk will help you to identify it. You will find the gastropod shell is on page 11—it's a Northern Rough Periwinkle.

5 **If you can't find the shell,** look through the pages for other kinds of shore. A shell from a sandy beach might have been carried by the tide to a rocky one. You will find the bivalve shell on page 13; it's a Blue Mussel.

6 **If you still can't find the shell,** try looking in the next-door area, or in a larger field guide (see page 78 for some suggestions). You may have picked up one that has been washed in from deep water or something very rare!

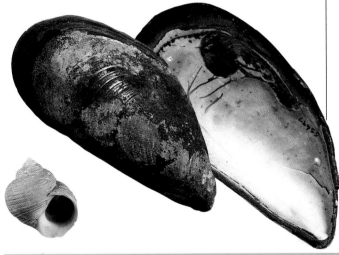

Top-of-page Picture Bands

Each habitat (type of beach) has a different picture band at the top of the page. These are shown below.

Estuaries and Lagoons

Sand and Mud Flats

Rocky Shores and Pools

Wood and Rock Borers

You will find two or three of these habitats in each of the four sections of this book.

What To Look For

Kinds of shells

Biologists divide mollusks into seven groups, called classes, but only some of them count as seashells.

GASTROPODS have a single shell. They include snails, periwinkles, whelks, and conches. Most have a coiled shell, although some (like limpets and slipper-shells) have a cap-shaped shell.

BIVALVES have two shells, or valves, hinged together. They include clams, oysters, and scallops.

TUSK SHELLS are open at both ends. They bury themselves in the sand with only the narrow end sticking out to suck in water.

CHITONS have eight shelly plates, binded together at the sides by a leather belt.

Parts of a shell

This is a gastropod shell. The shape of the different sections, the color, and their overall size will help you to identify gastropods.

The point of the shell is called the spire. It was the first part to be formed.

As the gastropod grew, it added a new whorl to the shell and moved into it. The number of whorls show how old the shell is.

The shell formed around this solid central pillar.

These ridges are called spiral cords.

The outer lip of the body whorl gets thicker as the gastropod gets older.

These ridges are called axial bands.

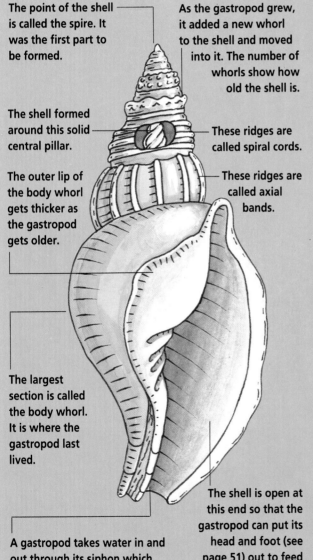

The largest section is called the body whorl. It is where the gastropod last lived.

The shell is open at this end so that the gastropod can put its head and foot (see page 51) out to feed and move about.

A gastropod takes water in and out through its siphon which reaches the outside here.

This is one half of a bivalve shell. The shape of the scars and the number of hinge teeth help to identify bivalves.

The hinge teeth allow the two valves to open and close.

The ligament holds the two valves of the mollusk together.

These scars show where the bivalve's adductor muscles gripped the shell. It used these muscles to keep the two halves closed.

The beak is the first bit of the shell to be formed.

A bivalve takes water in and out through its syphon. This dip in the pallial line shows where the muscles for the syphon were attached.

This scar is the pallial line. It shows where the mantle muscles were attached. The mantle contains the glands that form the shell.

The closed end of a bivalve shell

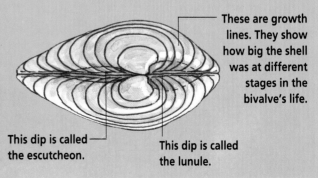

These are growth lines. They show how big the shell was at different stages in the bivalve's life.

This dip is called the escutcheon.

This dip is called the lunule.

Atlantic Coast: Labrador to Virginia

The section of Atlantic coastline that runs from Labrador to Virginia is fairly rich in shallow-water and shore species of mollusk. There is an enormous variation in types of shore, from the extensive, intertidal mud flats of the Bay of Fundy to the rocky coasts of Nova Scotia, and to the sandy beaches of Cape Cod.

Malacologists (shell collectors) divide the region into two provinces. The stretch from Labrador to Cape Cod is called the Acadian province, and from Cape Cod to Cape Hatteras is called the Virginian province.

New England has about 800 species of mollusks, but most of them are in offshore waters and are not often found on the beach. However, specimens are sometimes found washed up after storms, or abandoned by the receding tides.

Rock pools farther away from the ocean are generally less likely to have shells in them. If it is sunny for a long time, some of the water may evaporate and the remainder will become too salty for the mollusks. If there is a drenching rainstorm, it may dilute the seawater and make it too fresh. Mollusks like conditions to be just right.

Rocky Shores & Pools

Rocky shores have rough waves, but at low tide you can find limpets and periwinkles clinging to rocks, sometimes under hanging seaweeds. There is no better protected area for a group of mollusks and other sea creatures than the pools of clear seawater that are left by the receding tide.

Atlantic Plate Limpet

Limpets all live on rocks. Each limpet's shell grows to fit the patch of rock where it spends its time, so that when it settles down, not even the strongest wave can dislodge it. This limpet can be found clinging to rocks from the Arctic coasts to Long Island, New York. It has an oval shell, with the apex of its dome nearly in the center. The outside is a dull cream-gray with bars and streaks of brown. Inside it is a bluish white with a brown center.

Limpet family
About 1 ins long
First discovered by Mueller in 1776

Atlantic Dogwinkle

This spindle-shaped shell has a tall spire. The shell may be smooth or have spiral ridges. It is usually a dull white, but it may be yellowish and have dark-brown spiral bands. This winkle feeds on barnacles and small mussels; it lays its eggs in leathery capsules. It gives off a purple dye, which was once used for marking laundry. It is found from southern Labrador to New York.

Murex family – About 1½ ins long
First discovered by Linnaeus in 1758

Common Periwinkle

This is one of the largest periwinkles. This sea snail is common on intertidal rocks from northern Canada to Delaware. It has a solid, globular shell with a strong, thin outer lip. The color is a drab gray, sometimes with fine, spiral, white streaks. Like all periwinkles, this snail is a vegetarian.

Periwinkle family
About 1 ins long
First discovered by Linnaeus in 1758

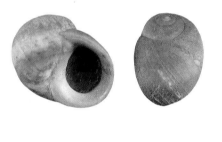

Northern Yellow Periwinkle

The solid, ball-shaped shell of this small periwinkle is usually a bright, brownish yellow, and may have a brown or white spiral band. It is flatter than many other periwinkles. These snails tend to hide under clumps of overhanging seaweeds, on which the female lays its jellylike egg masses. It is common from southern Labrador to New Jersey.

Periwinkle family
About ½ ins long
First discovered by Linnaeus·in 1758

Northern Rough Periwinkle

This periwinkle also has a solid shell, but is much more pointed in shape than the Northern Yellow Periwinkle. The surface is almost smooth, but has fine threads, and the color is gray with a darker pattern and a dark aperture. It is common from the Arctic seas to New Jersey. The females give birth to live young complete with shells.

Periwinkle family
About ½ ins long
First discovered by Olivi in 1792

Prickly Jingle Shell

Be careful if you pick this little shell up—the curved upper valve is often covered with small spines. The shell is very thin, but surprisingly strong. The lower shell is flat and has a small hole near the hinge. The mollusk pushes its strong byssus threads through this and uses them to attach itself to a rock. It is found from Labrador to North Carolina.

Jingle Shell family
About ¾ ins long
First discovered by Linnaeus in 1758

New England Nassa

This sea snail lives below the low tidemark, usually on clear sand, and eats dead fish and shrimps. The New England Nassa is common from Newfoundland to northern Florida. It has a knobby, pointed spiral shell with eight or nine whorls. The aperture has a thin outer lip.

Nassa Mud Snail family
About ¾ ins long
First discovered by Say in 1822

Eastern White Slipper-shell

This sea snail has a thin, white shell. It may be concave or convex, depending on what it grows. The snails gather on other dead shells, with one female and several males. If the female dies, one of the males turns into a female. It is very common from Canada to Texas.

Slipper-shell family
About 1¼ ins long
First discovered by Say in 1822

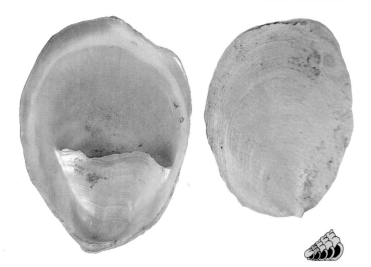

Common Atlantic Slipper-shell

Slipper-shells get their name from their peculiar shape, which is like a slipper or shoe. A shelly deck extends over the rear half of the inside of this shell. The outside of the shell ranges in color from dirty white to tan. Individuals usually stack up on one another, a female underneath and males on top. This shell is common from the maritime provinces of Canada to Texas.

Slipper-shell family
About 1½ ins long
First discovered by
Linnaeus in 1758

Blue Mussel

The Blue Mussel gets its name from its deep blue-black outer shell. The inner shell of this bivalve is a pearly white with a deep blue border. It is found in large colonies attached to intertidal rocks all down the eastern seaboard to South Carolina. At low tide it shuts its valves firmly to keep the moisture in.

Mussel family
About 2½ ins long
First discovered by
Linnaeus in 1758

Sand & Mud Flats

Sand and mud flats provide homes for many species of mollusks. They are only uncovered at low tide — don't confuse them with sandy beaches that slope into the water. Collect by following trails in the sand, or digging below clam holes.

A snail that lives in these habitats will use its large, single foot to creep across the sand. Many snails browse on fragments of edible material, animal, and vegetable, that are on the surface. Bivalves burrow into the sand or mud, leaving just their feeding siphons projecting. Many of them are filter feeders, drawing in water and filtering out edible particles from it.

Atlantic Bay Scallop

This is a common edible scallop, found at depths of 3–65 ft from the northern shore of Cape Cod south to New Jersey. It has a solid, almost circular shell with seventeen or eighteen low, rounded ribs. The color is usually a drab gray-brown, mottled with dark brown. The lower valve is slightly lighter than the upper one. The ears of the valves are of almost equal size.

Scallop family
About 2½ ins long
First discovered by Lamarck in 1819

Atlantic Nut Clam

This tiny, hard-shelled clam is common in sand and mud from Nova Scotia to Texas. It has a solid little shell, greenish gray with irregular, brownish rings. The outer shell has an oily iridescence. The inside of the shell is pearly. The hinge has many small teeth.

Nut Clam family
About ¼ ins long
First discovered by Say in 1822

Common Eastern Nassa

Mud flats from Cape Cod south to Texas are the home of this common, little mud snail. It has a a solid shell, colored gray-brown to whitish, with darker brown blotches. The outer lip of the aperture has four or five enamel teeth. Like other nassa mud snails it lives by scavenging.

Nassa Mud Snail family
About ½ ins long
First discovered by Say in 1822

Atlantic Surf Clam

This is a very common, edible species living in shallow water. It is dredged commercially offshore from Nova Scotia to North Carolina. It has a smooth shell, almost oval in shape, with a sunken pit in the center of the hinge. The color is yellowish white with a thin yellowish brown over-layer.

Surf Clam family
About 5 ins long
First discovered by Dillwyn in 1817

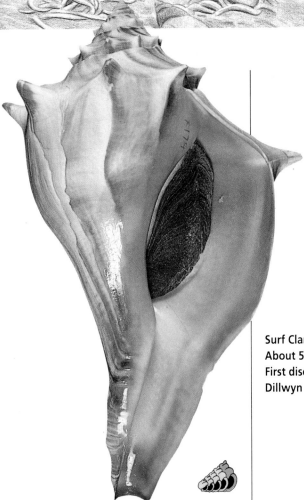

Knobbed Whelk

This huge snail is a meat-eater, which belongs to a family normally found in tropical waters. This common whelk feeds on clams. It lives in the shallow waters of the intertidal flats from Cape Cod south to North Carolina. It is named for its spines or knobs, and the shell has a right-handed twist. The aperture is a light orange-yellow, although some specimens are brick red.

Busycon Whelk family
About 7 ins long
First discovered by Gmelin in 1791

Common Northern Moon Snail

This is much larger than the spotted species, with a globular shell colored brownish gray to dirty white. The aperture is glossy tan-colored or marked with purplish brown stains. The egg case is a wide, circular ribbon of sand with tiny eggs embedded in it. It crumbles when dry. This snail is common from the Gulf of St Lawrence to North Carolina.

Moon Snail family
About 4 ins long
First discovered by Say in 1822

Sand & Mud Flats

Atlantic Razor Clam

Unlike most other razor clams, this one is not long and thin, but an elongated oval like a mussel. The shell is thin and delicate, and the over-layer of the shell has a greenish tinge. The inside is a glossy, purplish white, with a strong white rib. It burrows into firm sand from the Gulf of St Lawrence to North Carolina, and is very common.

Razor Clam family
About 2 ins long
First discovered by Say in 1822

Sanded Lyonsia

The tiny Sanded Lyonsia is named for the dusting of sand grains that are cemented to the over-layer of its shell. It belongs to a family of fragile clams that are usually distorted in shape, because they nestle in rock crevices, sponges, and peat. It is almost oblong in shape. It is fairly common from Greenland to Maine.

Lyonsia Clam family
About ½ ins long
First discovered by Mueller in 1842

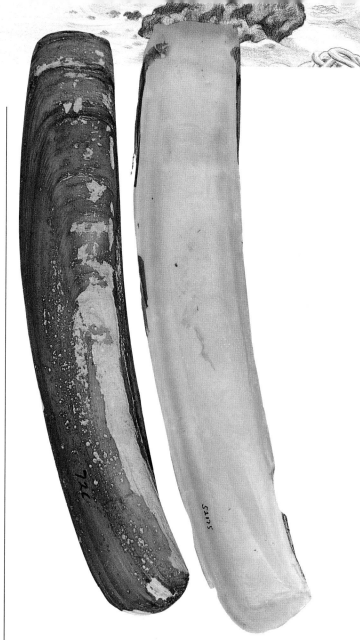

Atlantic Jackknife Clam

This very long clam looks like an old-fashioned cutthroat razor. It has a smooth shell, with the two valves forming a slightly curved cylinder. There are wide gapes (holes) at each end. The shell is basically white, with a varnishlike over-layer of brownish green. It is a common edible species, living in sand burrows from southern Labrador to South Carolina.

Razor Clam family
About 9 ins long
First discovered by Conrad in 1843

Chalky Macoma

The Chalky Macoma belongs to a family of bivalves known as tellins. Its shell is an elongated oval, with a gray over-layer, which is usually worn away except at the margins. The beak is not central, but about three-fifths of the way toward the back end. This is a common cold-water species, found offshore from Greenland to New York.

Tellin family – About 2 ins long
First discovered by Gmelin in 1791

Coquina

Coquina is a tiny clam with a wedge-shaped shell. From Maryland northward the color is dull-white with purple rays. In warmer waters the color varies considerably, but is usually bright. The coquina is found from New York to Texas. Unlike most clams, the clams of this group choose a habitat along wave-dashed, sandy beaches. They usually are found in large colonies.

Wedge Clam family
About ½ ins long
First discovered by
Say in 1822

Soft-shell Clam

This is an edible clam, very common in mud-flats or sandy flats from southern Labrador to North Carolina. It has a brittle, chalky shell. The shell gapes open at the rear end; this is where, in the live specimens, the siphon projects. People dig for these clams at low tide. Another name for this mollusk is the Sand-gaper.

Sand-gaper family – About 4 ins long
First discovered by Linnaeus in 1758

Gould's Pandora

This is a small, flat, cold-water clam. Its shell is compressed, and is shaped like a half-moon. The shell is thick, white, and chalky. In most specimens the shell is partly worn away to show the pearly under-layers. It is found from the Gulf of St Lawrence to North Carolina, in the intertidal region and downward.

Pandora Clam family
About 1 ins long
First discovered by
Dall in 1886

Estuaries & Salt Marsh

The waters of river estuaries are brackish, a mixture of salt water from the sea and fresh water from the river. Brackish water is also found in lagoons—shallow bodies of water close to the sea. Along the East Coast they are separated from the Atlantic Ocean by narrow strips of sand, called barrier islands. Only certain species of mussels and clams do well in brackish water, although oysters also enjoy this habitat. Wading birds, ducks and crabs feed on estuary mollusks.

Pointed Cingula

The Pointed Cingula belongs to a family of extremely small snails—so tiny that a teaspoon will hold dozens of them. There are hundreds of different species, and only experts can tell which is which. The Pointed Cingula is shown here as an example of how small these snails can be. It lives among seaweed in shallow, brackish water, from Nova Scotia to New Jersey.

Rissoid Snail family – About ⅛ ins long
First discovered by Gould in 1841

Solitary Paper-bubble

This small snail belongs to a group whose members are hermaphrodites—that is, each one is both male and female. It has a fragile shell, with the aperture extending the whole length. The color varies from translucent amber to whitish. It prefers a shallow, sandy area where it can hide among grasses; it lays its eggs on weed stems. Its range is from Cape Cod to North Carolina.

Bubble Shell family
About ½ ins long
First discovered by Say in 1822

Thick-lipped Drill

This is another common species that lives by boring into the shells of young oysters. It is slightly larger than the Atlantic Oyster Drill, with a more rugged-looking shell. The outer lip of the body whorl is thick, with raised teeth. It is found from south of Cape Cod to northern Florida.

Murex and Rock Shell family
About 1 ins long
First discovered by Say in 1822

Atlantic Oyster Drill

This little snail is the worst enemy of oysters. It drills a hole in the oyster's shell and eats the soft body. It destroys well over half the crop in some commercial oyster beds. It is a dirty gray or yellow in color, with a brown aperture. Its range is from Nova Scotia to northeastern Florida.

Murex and Rock Shell family
About 3/4 ins long – First discovered by Say in 1822

Baltic Macoma

The Baltic Macoma is a bivalve of the tellin family. It has a fairly small shell, oval, and moderately compressed. It is dull white in color, sometimes tinged with pink. The over-layer is thin and gray, and tends to flake off when dry. The Baltic Macoma is a very common intertidal and offshore species, found from Greenland to Georgia.

Tellin family – About 1 ins long
First discovered by Linnaeus in 1758

Conrad's False Mussel

This small, common bivalve belongs to a family of clams that have taken on the shape and habits of some mussels. It is found in brackish to fresh waters near rivers from New York to Texas. It attaches itself to rocks and twigs, in clumps that look like colonies of mussels. The over-layer of the shell is thin and somewhat glossy.

False Mussel family – About 3/4 ins long
First discovered by Conrad in 1831

Eastern American Oyster

The Eastern American Oyster is a large bivalve, with slightly wavy edges to its shells. The lower valve is cup-shaped, with a deep purple mark where the muscle was attached. The shape varies. It ranges from Cape Cod to Texas, and locally north to Maine and in the Gulf of St Lawrence. It survives being hunted by fish and other sea animals, and by humans, possibly because each female lays up to 500 million eggs a year.

Oyster family – About 5 ins long
First discovered by Gmelin in 1791

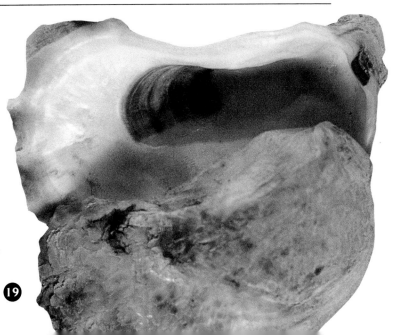

Northern Quahog

This is a large clam, almost as popular as oysters as a food. It is common in shallow, brackish water from Quebec to Texas. It is a bulky bivalve, gray with fine growth lines. The inside is white with purple stains. The Narragansett Indian word quahog (*say it*: co-hog) means "closed shell." Native Americans formerly used them as wampum, or a form of money. Another name for it is the Hardshell Clam.

Venus Clam family
About 4 ins long
First discovered by Linnaeus in 1758

Morrhua Venus

The small Morrhua Venus is also used as food—but by bottom-living fish, not by humans. The exterior of the somewhat bulky shell is dull gray to brownish red, with fine growth lines. It is found in shallow water from the Gulf of St Lawrence southward to North Carolina.

Venus Clam family
About 1 ins long
First discovered by Linsley in 1848

Amethyst Gem Clam

Dozens of these tiny clams fit into a teaspoon. They live under the sand in shallow water, from Nova Scotia southward to Texas. Sea birds and small fish eat large quantities of them. The outside of the thin shell is whitish tan or purple in color, and is covered with many fine furrows.

Venus Clam family
About ¼ ins long
First discovered by Totten in 1834

There are many salt marshes close to the sea, where the water is brackish. Meadows of tall grasses and reeds offer protection to several special kinds of mollusks, but they have to endure changing tides.

Eastern Melampus

This small snail breathes air, like the familiar garden snails. It is very common in salt marshes from eastern Quebec to Texas. It lives on grass stems, where it lays its jellylike egg masses. The snail is hermaphrodite (it is both male and female) and a vegetarian. Fresh shells are smooth, shining brown, and sometimes with three or four darker bands.

Marsh Snail family
About ½ ins long
First discovered by
Say in 1822

Marsh Periwinkle

This periwinkle lives in large numbers among the sedges of brackish marshes. It has a thick shell with many spiral grooves. It is grayish in color with short streaks of reddish brown on the spiral ridges. The aperture is reddish. It is found from New York to Texas.

Periwinkle family
About 1 ins long
First discovered by
Say in 1822

Eastern Mud Snail

This is a very common species on intertidal mud flats. It has a solid, smoothish shell with a high spire. The color is dark brown, with a narrow, tan band on the middle of the last whorl. The aperture is chocolate brown, and is one-third the length of the shell. The snail is found from Quebec to northeastern Florida.

Nassa Mud Snail family
About ¾ ins long
First discovered by Say in 1822

Atlantic Ribbed Mussel

This large, strong, but lightweight mussel is very common in intertidal grass and peat marshlands. Its range is from the Gulf of St Lawrence to northeastern Florida. The long shell is blackish brown, with strong, rough radial ribs. The inside is bluish white, flushed with purple at the wide end.

Mussel family
About 3 ins long
First discovered by Dillwyn in 1817

Explore the Shore

The shells you find depend on what kind of beach you explore. The best beaches to search are sandy and muddy ones for burrowing mollusks, and rocky ones for the mollusks that hide in crevices, cling to rocks, or are stranded in rock pools.

You will not find many shells on a shingle (pebble) beach, because the sea moves the stones about, smashing empty shells and making life impossible for living mollusks. At low tide the shingle dries out, which again is not a good habitat for sea-snails and bivalves.

Beach zones

You can divide every beach into five zones (shown below). They are governed by the rise and fall of the tide. High tide occurs every twelve hours and twenty-five minutes, and low tide is about six hours and thirteen minutes after high tide. You can find out from tide tables when the next low tide is due.

Roughly twice a month there are higher tides than usual. These are called **spring** tides, although they are nothing to do with the season of spring. In between the spring tides there are lower tides than usual, called **neap** tides. The shore between the highest point covered by spring tides and the lowest point uncovered by neap tides is the **intertidal** zone, and that is where you will do most of your exploring.

Make a beach map

If you are on the beach around low tide, why not make a map of the tidal zones? All you need is a long piece of string, a tape measure, a notebook, and a pencil.

1 **Tie one end of the string** to a rock or piece of driftwood and put it just above the line of trash that marks the edge of the splash zone.
2 **Tie the other end** to a rock or stick and place it at the edge of the water.

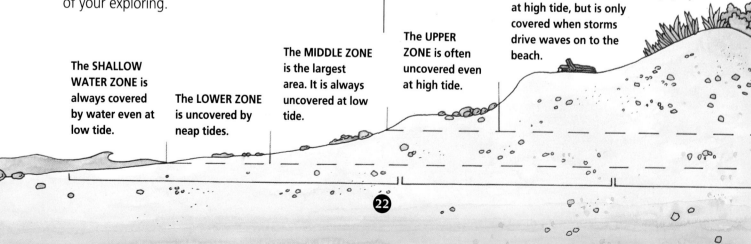

The SPLASH ZONE is wetted by spray at high tide, but is only covered when storms drive waves on to the beach.

The UPPER ZONE is often uncovered even at high tide.

The MIDDLE ZONE is the largest area. It is always uncovered at low tide.

The LOWER ZONE is uncovered by neap tides.

The SHALLOW WATER ZONE is always covered by water even at low tide.

Cockle Bay – 3rd June   Low Tide

3 yards Splash Zone	Periwinkles	Brown seaweed
7 yards Upper Zone	razorshell	Green seaweed
15 yards middle zone	oil	old rope	crab claw
10 yards Lower Zone	mussels	cockle

3 **Use pebbles or driftwood** to show where the different zones start.

4 **Measure each zone with the tape** and record how far it stretches.

5 **Make a list of what you find in each zone** — shells, sea weed, pollution items, (see right) and anything else of interest. Is there a band of pebbles or an outcrop of rocks?

6 **When you go to another beach** and do this survey again, compare the two maps to see how the beaches differ.

Pollution of our beaches is a major problem these days. Some is trash discarded by thoughtless people using the beaches, but a lot of trash comes from ships and is washed ashore. In some areas pollution is caused by sewage which has been pumped out to sea, but has then been washed back to the shore by the tide.

Pollution survey

It is a good exercise done by a group of you, to patrol a beach and make a list of what is on it that shouldn't be. Try to work out for yourself where the various kinds of pollution have come from. These are some of the things to look out for:

1 **Glass**: mostly bottles and often broken.

2 **Plastic and polyethylene**: plastic sometimes breaks up, but polyethylene bottles and bags don't.

3 **Wood**: some is washed down by rivers; the rest is from boats or old shore structures.

4 **Canisters and barrels**: these often still have their contents, which can range from chemicals to food. They don't always have a label to tell you what is inside. **Don't touch these,** but report them to the nearest coast guard or the police as soon as possible. **They may be dangerous.**

5 **Oil**: usually as patches of black tar, which can be very difficult to remove from your clothes. Use olive oil on a pad of cotton to clean up.

6 **Dead fish and sea birds**: these are usually victims of oil spillages.

7 **Wire, plain or barbed**.

8 **Bits of metal**, such as sheets of corrugated iron.

9 **Sewage**: this covers anything that goes down your toilet, plus disposable diapers.

Atlantic Coast: Carolina to Texas

This stretch of the North Atlantic coast is washed by warmer waters than the northern part, and so is home to many more species. In the southern part there are a number of tropical species, too.

Most of the cooler waters of the Carolina to Texas area have low, flat shorelines, where extensive stretches of estuaries, tidal flats and low salt marshes support many shallow-water mollusks. This area is known as the Carolinian province.

The long peninsula of Florida makes a break in the area. Its southern half and string of islands along the Lower Florida Keys are bathed by the warm waters of the Gulf Stream and West Indies. That is why this area has many Caribbean, tropical species of seashell and is part of the Caribbean province..

The climate varies from cool winters to hot summers. The winds are moderate except when the occasional hurricane may sweep up from the West Indies. Collecting during these rare storms is not a good idea, but after a strong wind there may be many shells on the beach.

Rocky Shores & Pools

Rocky shores and cliffs are unusual in this area, so you will not find limpets and periwinkles here. However, you will find rock pools. There is no better protected area for a group of mollusks than the pools of clear sea water left by the receding tide.

Common Jingle Shell

This jingle shell is commonly found attached to logs or dead shells from Cape Cod to Texas. It has a strong, smooth, thin shell, an irregular oval in shape. The upper valve is convex. The lower valve is flat, with a large hole near the hinge. The color is a translucent orange or yellow with a silvery sheen. When buried in mud, they turn black.

Jingle Shell family
About 1½ ins long
First discovered by Orbigny in 1842

Humphrey's Wentletrap

Humphrey's Wentletrap has a slender, thick shell, which is dull white. It has nine or ten convex whorls, each with eight or nine ribs. The outer lip of the aperture is rounded and thickened. It is common on sandy shores from Cape Cod to Texas.

Wentletrap family
About ¾ ins long
First discovered by Kiener in 1838

Brown-banded Wentletrap

This wentletrap can be distinguished by its moderately stout, whitish to yellowish shell, which is marked with two broad, brown bands on each whorl. A few shells are dark brown. There are twelve to eighteen ribs on each whorl. It is common from Cape Cod to Florida and Texas.

Wentletrap family
About ½ ins long
First discovered by Kurtz in 1860

Angulate Wentletrap

Wentletraps are tall, spirelike sea snails. The odd name comes from a Dutch word for a spiral staircase. The moderately stout shell of the Angulate Wentletrap is pure white. It has eight whorls with nine or ten thin ribs. It is very common, and may be found buried in the sand near the sea anemones on which it feeds. Its range is from New York to Texas.

Wentletrap family
About 1 ins long
First discovered by Say in 1830

Four-toothed Nerite

This nerite has a white, gaping mouth with four strong teeth. Its shell is a dirty white, with squarish black and red marks. It is common and is found clinging to intertidal rocks from southern Florida to Texas.

Nerite family
About ¾ ins long
First discovered by Gmelin in 1791

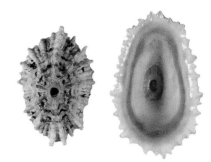

Cayenne Keyhole Limpet

Like other keyhole limpets, the Cayenne Keyhole Limpet has a keyhole-shaped hole near the apex of its single shell. It has many irregular radial ribs, every third or fourth being larger than the rest. The outside is dark gray, and the inside a paler gray. It is very common on rocks from New Jersey to Texas.

Keyhole Limpet family
About ¾ ins long
First discovered by Lamarck in 1822

Bleeding Tooth

The Bleeding Tooth gets its name from its aperture, which has white teeth on a light red background. It has a solid, sturdy shell. Like other members of its family, it is a sea snail of tropical waters. It is very common clinging to intertidal rocks, and may be found above the high tidemark.

Nerite family
About 1 ins long
First discovered by Linnaeus in 1758

Chestnut Latirus

Its color, a rich chestnut-brown, gives this spindle its name. The light-colored aperture has fine white threads. The shell is stubbier than many other spindles, with nine large nodules on the shoulder of each whorl. It is common on rocks at low tide from Florida to Texas.

Spindle family
About 1½ ins long
First discovered by Linnaeus in 1791

Tulip Mussel

This mussel clings to rocks and broken shells. It is an offshore bivalve, washed ashore after storms. It is common on beaches from North Carolina to Florida and Texas. The shell is light brown, with a brown, sometimes hairy over-layer. The inside of the shell is white stained with blue, brown, or rose.

Mussel family
About 2 ins long
First discovered by Leach in 1815

Zebra Ark

Ark clams are bivalves that have file-like teeth along the hinge. The Zebra Ark is much longer than it is deep, and has brown and white zebra-like stripes. It flourishes attached to rocks, often covered with other marine growths. You may find it washed ashore after a storm. It is common from North Carolina to Texas.

Ark Clam family
About 3 ins long
First discovered by Swainson in 1833

Sentis Scallop

This little scallop lives attached to the underside of rocks in the intertidal zone. Its valves are nearly flat and have about fifty ribs. One ear is prominent, the other is very small. Its bright colors vary greatly. It is common from North Carolina to the Caribbean.

Scallop family
About 1 ins long
First discovered by Reeve in 1853

Transverse Ark

The left valve of the Transverse Ark overlaps the smaller right valve. The shell is covered with a grayish brown over-layer. The shell has thirty to thirty-five ribs, usually beaded on the left valve, but only rarely on the right valve. It is common in sandy mud below the low tidemark.

Ark Clam family – About 1 ins long
First discovered by Say in 1822

Kitten's Paw

The high, rounded ribs of this small scallop give it its popular name, and give it a wavy margin. The shell is thick. The hinge has two strong pegs in the upper valve, which fit into sockets in the lower valve. It is common, and is found attached to rocks and shells in the intertidal zone, from North Carolina southward.

Kitten's Paw family – About 1 ins long
First discovered by Lamarck in 1801

Zigzag Periwinkle

This little periwinkle has a gray shell. There are twenty to twenty-five fine, reddish, wavy lines on each whorl, for which it is named. It is common in rock crevices on the shores of southeastern Florida.

Periwinkle family
About ½ ins long
First discovered by Gmelin in 1791

Sand & Mud Flats

Sand and mud flats provide homes for many species of mollusks. They are only uncovered at low tide — don't confuse them with sandy beaches that slope into the water. Collecting can be very good, especially by following trails in the sand, or digging below clam holes.

A snail that lives in these habitats will use its large, single foot to creep across the sand. Many browse on fragments of animal and vegetable material on the surface. Bivalves burrow into the sand or mud, leaving just their feeding siphons projecting. Many are filter feeders, drawing in water and filtering out edible particles from it.

Shark Eye

The Shark Eye is named for its appearance, owing to the buttonlike, brown callus on its otherwise glossy, gray, globular shell. It is one of a family, known as moon snails, that eat clams. It is common on sand flats from Massachusetts to Texas. Its egg mass is a sandy collar.

Moon Snail family
About 2½ ins long
First discovered by Say in 1822

Common Baby's Ear

The Common Baby's Ear is also a moon snail. It has a flat white shell, with a very large aperture. The shell is covered with fine spiral lines. The animal, which fully envelops the shell when alive, feeds on small bivalves. It is common in the shallow, sandy waters of the southeastern United States.

Moon Snail family
About 1½ ins long
First discovered by Say in 1832

Tesselate Nerite

The Tesselate Nerite gets its name from the small black dots on its dirty white shell, which look like a Roman tessellated (or mosaic) pavement. It is common in intertidal rock pools from Florida to Texas.

Nerite family
About ½ ins long
First discovered by Gmelin in 1791

Blood Ark

This shell is named for the red color of the living animal. The shell is white and has a blackish brown over-layer, hairy and fairly thick. It has twenty-six to thirty-five smooth ribs. The Blood Ark is common in shallow waters from Cape Cod to Texas.

Ark Clam family
About 2 ins long
First discovered by Bruguière in 1789

Ponderous Ark

The Ponderous Ark, as its name implies, has a solid, heavy shell. The valves are the same size, and their beaks point backward. The twenty-seven to thirty-one ribs are square, with a fine-cut line down them. It is common in warm waters from Virginia to Texas.

Ark Clam family
About 2 ins long
First discovered by Say in 1822

Purplish Tagelus

The valves of this razor clam form a broad, flattened cylinder. They are fragile and smooth. The color is whitish purple, with a very thin, glossy, brown over-layer. The clam is common on sand flats from Massachusetts south to Texas and beyond.

Tagelus Razor Clam family
About 1½ ins long
First discovered by Spengler in 1794

False Tulip Mussel

This mussel is smaller than the Tulip Mussel, which is found in rocky, shallow waters. It has a strong, oblong, swollen shell. The outside is brownish purple, with a whitish ray. It is a sub-species of a cold-water mussel, and is commonly found in shallow water off the southeastern United States.

Mussel family
About 2 ins long
First discovered by Beauperthuy in 1967

Florida Fighting Conch

Like all conchs (*say it*: konks), this one eats red seaweed. It moves forward in a series of hops, using its sickle-shaped operculum (or trap-door) as a vaulting pole. Its eyes are on the ends of short stalks. The thick outer lip of the shell flares outward, and there are short spines on the spire. It is common in shallow water from North Carolina to Texas and beyond.

Conch family
About 3 ins long
First discovered by Gmelin in 1791

Common Fig Shell

This sea snail has a long, thin, conical shell, with the aperture running almost its full length. The spire is very flat. Thin criss-cross lines cover the outer surface. It can sometimes be mistaken for the heavy Pear Whelk (opposite). It feeds on sea urchins and related animals. It is common from North Carolina to Texas and beyond, in shallow water over sand.

Fig Shell family – About 3 ins long
First discovered by Roeding in 1798

Chestnut Turban

Turban family
About 1½ ins long
First discovered by Gmelin in 1791

Like other turbans, the Chestnut Turban is a warm and shallow water mollusk, feeding on seaweed. It has a heavy shell with beading; it sometimes has tiny spines as well. It is common offshore in shallow bays from North Carolina south to Texas and beyond.

Flamingo Tongue

The outside of this stout, glossy shell is cream with orange edges. The aperture runs the length of the shell. In the living creature the mantle extends to cover the shell completely. The mantle is spectacular — it is a light peach in color, speckled with orange dots rimmed in black. The snail is common on sea fans in shallow water from Florida to the islands of the West Indies.

Cyphoma Snail family
About 1 ins long
First discovered by Linnaeus in 1758

Scotch Bonnet

The square spots on the shell of the Scotch Bonnet form a pattern that slightly resembles a Scottish tartan, which is how it got its name. The whorls have spiral grooves and beaded cords. It lives in shallow, tropical waters. The female lays a tower of eggs, on which she perches. The shell is found washed ashore in the Carolinas and western Florida. It is the state shell of North Carolina.

Bonnet and Helmet Shell family
About 3 ins long – First discovered by Born in 1778

Pear Whelk

The Pear Whelk has a right-handed shell, usually with smooth, rounded shoulders. The color is pale, with a tan-colored, fuzzy over-layer. It is common from North Carolina to Texas.

Busycon Whelk family
About 5 ins long
First discovered by Lamarck in 1816

Sand & Mud Flats

Broad-ribbed Cardita

This little clam has a heavy, solid shell, with twenty raised, beaded radial ribs. The over-layer of the shell is gray. It is very common in shallow water from southern Florida to Texas and beyond.

Cardita Clam family – About 1 ins long
First discovered by Conrad in 1838

Florida Cone

The Florida Cone's range is from the Carolinas round to the western coast of Florida. It is another colorful shell, and comes in a variety of shades, often white with bands or patches of orange or yellow. Like all cones, it has tiny teeth on its tongue, from which it can inject poison into its prey. It is common on sandy flats.

Cone Shell family – About 1 ins long
First discovered by Gabb in 1868

Prickly Cockle

The Prickly Cockle is named for its twenty-seven or more prominent prickly ribs. The two valves are well-domed and elongated from the beak end. The color is white with brownish markings. The inside of the shell has bright pink and purple markings.

Cockle family – About 2½ ins long
First discovered by Shuttleworth in 1856

Common Dove-shell

There are many variations in the color of this tiny snail, but the most common colors are white and brown. The shell is squat and heavy, and has a thick outer lip. The snail is common in shallow water, and is often found on the seaweeds on which it feeds. Its range is from southeastern Florida to the islands of the West Indies.

Dove-shell family – About ¼ ins long
First discovered by Linnaeus in 1758

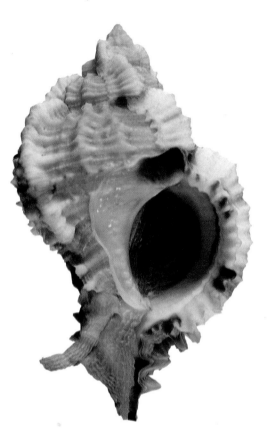

Atlantic Auger

The Atlantic Auger is long and narrow. The whorls are separated by a lighter spiral band. The color is light gray, banded with reddish brown and grayish purple. It can be found from Virginia to Texas and lives on sand in shallow water. Like cones, augers have a poison tooth and are carnivorous.

Auger Shell family
About 1½ ins long
First discovered by Say in 1822

Apple Murex

A strong, spiny shell is the clue to identifying the Apple Murex, a predator of bivalves and a scavenger of freshly dead sea animals. None of the spines is very long. There is yellow, tan, or orange near the inner lip of the aperture, and the outer lip has brown spots. It is common in shallow water in the south-eastern United States.

Murex family
About 2½ ins long
First discovered by Gmelin in 1791

Purplish Semele

You need to go to tropical waters to find the most colorful semele clams, but the Purplish Semele is a very good example. The colors are bright and vary from purple to orange, while the inside is glossy, and purple, brown, or orange. The shell is thin, but strong, with fine growth lines. It is common from North Carolina to Texas and beyond.

Semele Clam family
About 1¼ ins long
First discovered by Gmelin in 1791

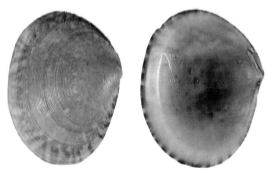

Collecting Expedition

To make your expedition a success you need the right clothing and equipment. It doesn't really matter what you wear as long as it suits the weather. Remember that the sun at the beach can be very strong, and you can easily be burned. So you should use a sun-screen cream, and may need to wear a thin T-shirt and sun-hat. Read the Collector's Code (page 2) before you start.

However, it is important what you put on your feet. On soft sand and mud it's fun to go barefoot, but a lot of litter is washed on to beaches these days, and it can include sharp objects such as cans, broken glass, and jagged pieces of plastic. On rocky beaches the rocks themselves can cause cuts, so always have boots or shoes with you.

Where to look

On a rocky shore you can find live limpets and periwinkles clinging to rocks. You will also find barnacles and mussels there, and the sea-snails that prey on them, such as whelks.

Some periwinkles hide in cracks in the rocks. If a mollusk has burrowed into the rock by drilling a hole, it is probably a piddock (see pages 74–77). Other piddocks, and the destructive shipworms, bore into wood. Examine pieces of driftwood to see if you can find them.

Equipment

The following equipment is useful for finding specimens, examining and recording them, and taking them home.

1 **A spade or trowel** is essential on sand and mud to dig up live burrowing mollusks.
2 **A kitchen strainer** to strain out very small shells from sand or mud.
3 **A clear plastic box** to inspect pools with on windy days.
4 **A good magnifying glass** to examine specimens closely. Buy one of the small folding type with a magnification of x 10.
5 **A field notebook** to keep a record of what you find and where (see opposite).
6 **A waterproof pen.**
7 **A plastic bucket**, with a tight lid is best, for transporting live specimens. Fill it with seawater.
8 **Small plastic bags** for empty shells.
9 **A light backpack** to carry everything in.

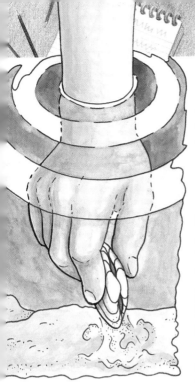

Jetties, posts, and piers on sand beaches are also worth checking for piddocks and mussels.

If you pick up a live mollusk to examine it you should put it back afterward where you found it. If you want to take it home, turn to pages 50–1 which explain how to care for live mollusks.

Live bivalves are generally hiding in burrows in sand or mud. This is where you will need your spade to dig them out. It is not an easy task, and razor shells in particular are more skilled at hiding than you will be at finding them. You are just as likely to uncover marine worms. It will pay you to sieve the sand or mud as you dig, because so many mollusks are tiny.

Be prepared to turn over rocks or peer under them. Some sea-snails live on seaweeds, and are probably on the under side, but always roll them back after you have looked.

Use the clear plastic box to look in rock pools on windy days without disturbing the occupants. You can often find a rich haul of mollusks which have been exposed as the tide goes out. Check under the overhang of the rocks, and lift up seaweeds.

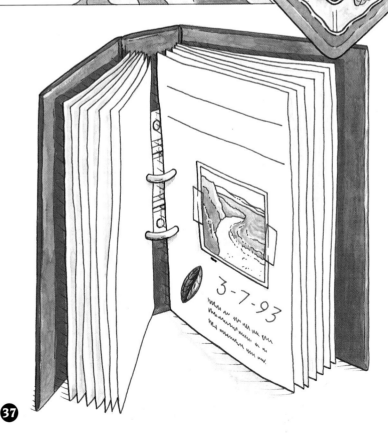

Keeping a record

Your field notebook is essential for recording how and where you found shells, and any interesting information about the beach and the nearby area.

1 **When you go to a new beach**, give it a special number and make a note of the date and what sort of habitats it has (rock pools, sand flats, etc). Why not take a photo for your record file (right)?

2 **Each time you visit** that beach, record where the tide was and what the weather was like.

3 **When you find a mollusk or an empty shell**, make a note of the habitat in which you found it, whether any other mollusks were around, and what other creatures or features were nearby.

4 **Write the beach's special number** on the outside of each bag, add the date, and number the bag as well. Use the same bag number in your notebook, so that you can match up your notes to the bags.

Estuaries & Salt Marsh

The waters of river estuaries are brackish, a mixture of salt water from the sea and fresh water from the river. Brackish water is also found in lagoons—shallow bodies of water close to the sea. Along the eastern coast they are separated from the Atlantic Ocean by narrow strips of sand, called barrier islands. Only certain species of mussels and clams do well in brackish water, although oysters also enjoy this habitat. Wading birds, ducks and crabs feed on estuary mollusks.

Lunar Dove-shell

In spite of its tiny size, this snail is an aggressive carnivore. It belongs to a family most of whose members live in tropical waters. The Lunar Dove-shell has a smooth, translucent, glossy shell. It is gray with brown or yellow stripes. It is a very common shallow-water species, especially in weedy areas of estuaries, from Massachusetts south to Texas and beyond.

Dove-shell family
About ¼ ins long
First discovered by Say in 1826

Hooked Mussel

This small mussel is named for its distinctive shape. The shell is flattish and wide, with many waxy axial ribs. The outside is a dark grayish brown. The inside is purplish to rosy-brown, with a narrow blue-grey border. The mussel is common, often on wood piling, in brackish water from Cape Cod to Texas and beyond.

Mussel family
About 1½ ins long
First discovered by Rafinesque in 1820

Pointed Nut Clam

This is a tiny clam, whose shell is rounded at the front end and pointed at the rear. It has concentric rings, evenly sized and evenly spaced. It is white, with a thin, yellow over-layer. It is common in sandy mud under shallow water from Cape Cod to Texas and beyond.

Nut Clam family
About ¼ ins long
First discovered by Conrad in 1831

Morton's Egg Cockle

This cockle is thin-shelled, small, swollen and oval, and not very big. It has a smooth, glossy shell, yellowish brown on the outside with darker zigzag markings. Inside it is a bright yellow, which rapidly fades. It is a common food for ducks. Its range is from Cape Cod to Texas.

Cockle family
About 1 ins long
First discovered by Conrad in 1830

Convex Slipper-shell

This little slipper-shell is almost a perfect oval. Most are highly arched, and the color is a dark brown, reddish to purplish in tinge. Some specimens may be spotted. Many shells are thick and heavy. Others, found attached to other shells, are fragile. Slipper-shells that settle on eelgrass grow long, narrow shells. Their range is from Massachusetts to Texas and the West Indies.

Slipper-shell family
About ½ ins long
First discovered by Say in 1822

Tenta Macoma

This small tellin clam has a fragile shell, shaped like an elongated oval. The rear end is slightly twisted to the left. The outside is white, with a delicate iridescence. Inside, the shell is a glossy white tinged with yellow. It is common from Cape Cod south to Florida.

Tellin family
About ¾ ins long
First discovered by Say in 1837

The southeastern coasts of the United States are particularly rich in brackish lagoons and salt marshes. They are home to those mollusks that thrive in a habitat of brackish water and warm climate. In Florida and the Gulf of Mexico, mangrove trees grow at the edge of these lagoons.

Stout Tagelus

The Stout Tagelus is a razor clam, living in sand under shallow water. It has an oblong shell, almost a cylinder, and gaping. The exterior is smoothish, with tiny, irregular scratches. The over-layer is brownish yellow, while the inside is whitish. It is moderately common from Cape Cod south to Texas and beyond.

Tagelus Razor Clam family
About 3 ins long
First discovered by Lightfoot in 1786

Common Atlantic Marginella

Like other margin shells, this one is able to move over the shallow sea bottom very quickly, despite its small size. The spire is stubby, and the shell is very glossy, and golden or orange-brown in color. In the Florida Keys you may find a gray variety. A few of these little snails have left-handed shells. They are very common in sandy-bottomed shallow areas from North Carolina to Texas and beyond.

Margin Shell family – About 1/4 ins long
First discovered by Menke in 1828

West Indian Bubble

There are several species of these shells. Some are strong, others fragile; some are cylindrical, others bulbous. This species is smooth, white with brownish markings. Like other bubble shells, this snail is hermaphrodite (each animal is both male and female.) It is common on grassy mud flats from North Carolina to southeastern Florida.

Bubble Shell family
About 3/4 ins long
First discovered by
Bruguière in 1792

Long-spined Star Shell

Like other turban snails, the Long-spined Star Shell has a heavy shell. This snail is found in southeastern Florida, hiding in grassy shallows. It can be identified by its many spines, and the generally low spire. Seen from above, it looks like a many-rayed star, which is how it got its name.

Turban family
About 1½ ins long
First discovered by Roeding in 1798

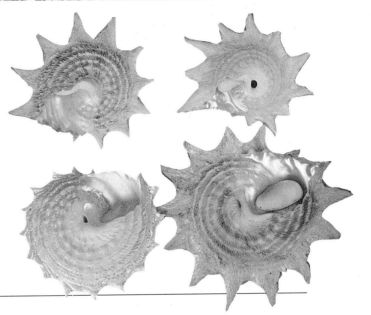

Angulate Periwinkle

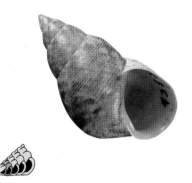

The Angulate Periwinkle is one of a group of similar species which live in the Gulf of Mexico and the Caribbean Sea. It is a thin, strong shell, which is nearly smooth, but has many fine spiral lines. The color varies,but the aperture is whitish. It is common from southern Florida to Texas and beyond, and is often found in mangrove trees.

Periwinkle family – About 1 ins long
First discovered by Lamarck in 1822

Carolina Marsh Clam

The Carolina Marsh Clam is commonly found in river estuaries from Virginia to northern Florida, and in Texas. It has a strong, bulbous shell, usually worn away at the beaks of the valves. The over-layer is a glossy brown, covered with tiny, shining scales.

Marsh Clam family
About 1¼ ins long
First discovered by Bosc in 1801

41

Pacific Coast: Alaska to Oregon

The Pacific coast of the United States supports its own kinds of mollusks. As in the East, the terrain and climate vary considerably. Alaska and British Columbia, the northernmost part of the continent, have a long coastline with hundreds of bays, fiords, and other inlets, many of them rocky.

While the climate is generally cold, southern Alaska is warmed by the Japan Current and the winds that blow over it. Glaciers and rivers flow into these waters from the bleak Alaskan mountain regions. The area is called the Aleutian province.

The coastlines of southern British Columbia, Washington, and Oregon are generally rugged, with many miles of cliffs close to the shore and with rocky beaches. Sandy beaches are found between high headlands and there are many river estuaries. The Oregonian province extends south to central California.

The waters of the Pacific Ocean in this region vary from cool to cold. Not surprisingly, the area is dominated by rock-dwelling species of sea snails, cold-water whelks, and Arctic clams. Edible shellfish —like clams, oysters and scallops—are very common in the south of this region.

Rocky Shores & Pools

Rocky shores have rough waves, but at low tide you can find mollusks clinging to rocks, or sometimes under hanging seaweeds. There is no better protected area for a host of mollusks and other sea creatures than the pools of clear salt water left behind by the receding tide. The northern Pacific coast of America is one of the best places in the world to hunt for shells. It is crowded with limpets, which are essentially a cold-water family.

All limpets live on rocks. Each limpet's shell grows to fit the patch of rock where it spends its time, so that when it settles down, not even the strongest wave can dislodge it. Often the rim of the shell wears into the rock slightly, making an even better fit. Limpets may wander around at night or at high tide to graze on algae, but return in the morning to their home patch.

File Limpet

This limpet has a low apex to its shell, which varies from elliptical to almost circular. It is covered with rows of beads forming tiny radial ribs. The outside is greenish black. Inside, the shell is a glossy white, tinged with blue, and often has patches of brown with a solid band of brown near the edge. It is common from Puget Sound in Washington down to southern California.

American Limpet family
About 1¼ ins long
First discovered by Carpenter in 1864

Fenestrate Limpet

You will find the Fenestrate Limpet among loose boulders set in sand. It feeds only at high tide. The shell is almost round, high, and smoothish. As far south as Oregon it is a plain, dark gray, but Californian species are gray-green with cream spots. The inside has a brown central spot. This limpet is common from Alaska south to California.

American Limpet family
About 1¼ ins long
First discovered by Reeve in 1855

Seaweed Limpet

As its name suggests, the Seaweed Limpet is found on large kelps. It has a small, solid shell, with a high spire. It is twice as long as it is wide. It is a uniform, greasy, light brown. A similar-looking species, the Black Limpet, is black inside and out, and clings to several kinds of large snails. Both limpets are very common from Alaska to Baja California, Mexico.

American Limpet family
About ½ ins long
First discovered by Hinds in 1842

Mask Limpet

This limpet is common from Alaska to northern California. It lives on rocks where waves wash out the crevices where it hides. It feeds mostly during low tides at night. The shell is a longish oval; it has a fairly high apex pointing forward, and about one-third of the way from the front edge. The outside is dark gray with a fine pattern of white squares and triangles. Inside the shell is bluish white to blackish blue in color.

American Limpet family – About 1¼ ins long
First discovered by Rathke in 1833

Pacific Plate Limpet

From Alaska to Oregon this limpet is common on rocky shores, but it is rare further south. It has a flat, smoothish, almost circular shell, with the apex near the center. The outside is greenish gray, mottled or banded in slate gray. The inside is bluish white, with alternating bands of blackish brown and bluish gray around the rim.

American Limpet family – About 1½ ins long
First discovered by Rathke in 1833

Shield Limpet

This limpet is common in the intertidal zone from Alaska to Mexico. It has a strong elliptical shell, with a high apex near the center. There are about twenty-five small ribs, and the edge of the shell is slightly wavy. The outside is creamy-gray, with strong black stripes. The inside is mostly a pale bluish white.

American Limpet family – About 1¼ ins long
First discovered by Rathke in 1833

Rough Keyhole Limpet

The outside of the shell is covered with rough radial threads, which is how this limpet got its name. The keyhole is almost round, and is located slightly toward the front. The outside is grayish white with purplish blue radial bands. The inside is bluish white. This limpet is commonly found on rocks from the low tidemark downward, or on the stalks of kelp. It is found from Cook's Inlet, Alaska, to southern California.

Keyhole Limpet family – About 1½ ins long
First discovered by Rathke in 1833

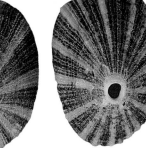

Carpenter's Dwarf Turban

This is one of the few turban snails to live in cold water, most of the rest of the family being tropical. It is frequently washed ashore from Alaska to Baja California, Mexico. It has a small, solid globular shell, varying in color from pinkish to brownish red. The last whorl and the base have between fifteen and twenty evenly-sized, smooth spiral cords.

Turban Snail family
About ³/₄ ins long
First discovered by Pilsbry in 1888

Trochoid Shell family
About ¹/₂ ins long
First discovered by Gould in 1849

Puppet Margarite

The shell of this snail is top-shaped, with a moderately-high spire, often eroded at the tip. The shell has five or six whorls. The color of the shell varies from chalky white to yellowish gray. The aperture is rosy or greenish, and like all snails of this family, the inside is pearly. The snail is common from Alaska to Oregon, but not so common south to San Diego, California.

Western Ribbed Top-shell

This top-shell has a solid and heavy shell with well-rounded whorls. The background color is dark chocolate, covered with six to eight, smooth, light-brown cords. Occasional specimens have a mauve tinge. The aperture is pearly-white. It is very common among stones and algae from Alaska to northern California, but is rare further south.

Trochoid Snail family
About ³/₄ ins long
First discovered by Gould in 1849

Black Tegula

The head and tentacles of this snail are completely black. In males the sole of the foot is usually light cream, while that of females is brown. The heavy, solid shell is a dark purple-brown, and is usually smooth. The snail is a very common rock-dwelling species from Vancouver, British Columbia, to southern California.

Trochoid Snail family
About 1¹/₂ ins long
First discovered by Adams in 1855

Checkered Periwinkle

This little sea-snail has a longish shell with a pointed spire. The shell is smooth and almost glossy. The color ranges from light to dark reddish brown. It often has irregular spots of bluish white, giving it a checked appearance. It is common in the upper intertidal zone, from Kodiak Island, Alaska, to California.

Periwinkle family
About ½ ins long
First discovered by Gould in 1849

Joseph's Coat Amphissa

This little snail is common in the intertidal zone from British Columbia to Baja California, Mexico. Although small, it is an aggressive carnivore. It has an elongated shell, which is thin but strong, with seven glossy whorls. The whorls have about fifteen slanting axial ribs. The color is pinkish gray, mottled with orange-brown.

Dove-shell family
About ½ ins long
First discovered by Dall in 1871

Oregon Triton

Most tritons are large and live in warm waters, but the Oregon Triton is common in cold water near the shore, from Alaska to British Columbia. It is found in deeper water south to San Diego, California. The shell is spindle-shaped, and covered with a thick, fuzzy, heavy over-layer of grayish brown. The aperture is white. All tritons are carnivorous.

Triton family
About 3 ins long
First discovered by
Redfield in 1848

Lurid Dwarf Triton

The Lurid Dwarf Triton is carnivorous, like all shells that live on rocks. It is very common in intertidal areas from southern Alaska to northern California, but is rarer further south. The shell is top-shaped, with an elongated spire, rounded whorls, and many rough spiral cords. The color varies from whitish to a rusty brown. The over-layer is fuzzy and dark brown.

Rock Shell family
About 1 ins long
First discovered by Middendorff in 1848

Frilled Dogwinkle

The shape and color of this rock-dwelling shell vary considerably. Some specimens have a smooth outline, while in others the whorls are clearly stepped. The shell may be white, grayish, cream, or orange. The snail is very common on rocks from the Bering Strait down to central California.

Rock Shell family
About 2 ins long
First discovered by Gmelin in 1791

File Dogwinkle

This is a common cold-water species, found in the intertidal zone. It ranges from Japan through Alaska down to northern California. It is roughly spindle-shaped with a low spire, and the rounded whorls have between seventeen and twenty spiral cords. The outside is whitish or orange-brown.

Rock Shell family
About 1¼ ins long
First discovered by Gmelin in 1791

Emarginate Dogwinkle

This shell is found in many variations: the spire may be high or low, while the color varies from rusty brown to a dirty gray. The aperture is light brown, and the whorls are covered with coarse spiral cords. This is a very common rock-dwelling species of snail, ranging from Alaska to southern California.

Rock Shell family
About 1 ins long
First discovered by Deshayes in 1839

Dire Whelk

A solid, spindle-shaped shell encloses this snail. It has nine to eleven, low axial ribs on the body whorl, and a sharp spire. The aperture is a little over half the length of the shell, and colored tan. The outer lip of the aperture has many short teeth inside the outer lip. This is a common shallow-water species ranging from Alaska as far south as Monterey in California.

Buccinum Whelk family
About 1 ins long
First discovered by Reeve in 1846

You are most likely to find these four mollusks trapped in rock pools. They are chitons and look something like a cross between a tortoise and a pill bug. Like pill bugs, they can curl up if dislodged from the rocks where they live. Most chitons are vegetarians.

Chitons have a shell formed of eight overlapping valves, or plates, bound together by a leathery girdle. A chiton's flat foot occupies most of the underside, and the small head has a mouth with radular teeth, but no tentacles. Instead of eyes a chiton has sensory cells, called aesthetes, which detect light.

Merten's Chiton

Merten's Chiton is oval in shape. Its color varies, but it is commonly yellowish with dark red streaks. Ribs and ridges on the plates give them an appearance like a net. The girdle has alternating yellow and reddish bands, and is covered with tiny scales looking like split peas. This chiton is very common in shallow water on hard surfaces from the Aleutian Islands, Alaska, to Baja California, Mexico.

Chiton class
About 1½ ins long
First discovered by Middendorff in 1847

Northern Red Chiton

The plates are rounded in shape, and their upper surface is smooth except for fine growth wrinkles. The color is light tan, with orange-red marbling. The girdle is reddish brown, covered with tiny scales. It is common on hard surfaces at depths of 10–660 feet, and is found from the Bering Strait to northern California and also from Greenland to Connecticut.

Chiton class
About 1 ins long
First discovered by Linnaeus in 1767

Lined Red Chiton

The plates of this chiton are smooth and shiny. Their color is orange to deep red, with oblique black lines bordered with white. The shells are white inside. The girdle is bare. This chiton is common in shallow water from Alaska south to California.

Chiton class
About 1¼ ins long
First discovered by Wood in 1815

Mossy Mopalia

The stiff hairs on the girdle, looking like a fringe of moss, give this chiton its name. Its shape varies from oblong to oval. The color can be a dull brown, blackish olive or gray. There are many varieties. This is a common intertidal species, ranging along the entire Pacific coast from Alaska to Baja California, Mexico.

Chiton class
About 1½ ins long
First discovered by Gould in 1846

Studying Live Mollusks

If you take live specimens home to study, you must have a suitable place to keep them. Never keep them away from their natural habitat for more than a week and only study a few at a time.

The shorter the time you keep them the better. One reason for this is that it is difficult to arrange a suitable supply of food for a mollusk unless you know exactly what it eats. If in doubt always ask somebody who knows, like your biology teacher or a more experienced collector.

You can observe sea snails in large glass jars, and you may find it as well to keep predatory animals, such as whelks, on their own in this way. You can feed them mussels or small clams. Thawed frozen shrimps are also enjoyed by carnivores. **Don't feed them more than once or twice a week** and remove the food that is not eaten that evening.

A seawater aquarium

The best place to keep specimens is in a regular aquarium. You can buy one in a pet store that specializes in fish tanks. Such a tank should be large enough to allow for a good layer of sand or gravel on the bottom — a four or six gallon tank is large enough.

Concentrate on specimens of species that require a similar environment. When you want to study something that needs a different habitat you should clean out the tank and start again.

The dealer who sells you the tank should advise you on what else you need. The equipment may include a filter, but this may remove the small algae that bivalves eat; and an air pump, to make sure the water has enough oxygen in it. (Sea animals absorb oxygen from the water, just as you do from the air you breathe.)

Because you are studying saltwater specimens, you will need to have enough sea water to fill the tank. Ask an adult to take a supply home for you by car, in a watertight container.

Mark the water level on the side of the aquarium and when it goes down, you can top it up with rain or pond water. Put a sheet of glass or plastic over the tank to stop the water evaporating, but leave a crack for air to circulate.

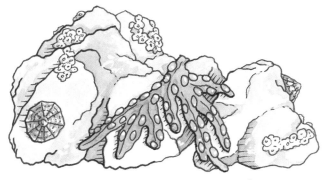

Decorating your aquarium

Try to create a realistic environment for your mollusks. Rocks with algae on them, from the seaside, will appeal to many sea snails, such as periwinkles and provide food. Some seaweed will help the appearance of the tank, and also help to provide a balanced environment.

Aquariums always function best with a layer of clean pea-gravel in the bottom. But if you want to study a mollusk that lives in mud or sand you will have to add a solid layer of sand in at least part of the tank, for them to burrow into. This should be 1–2 inches deep.

The water in a saltwater aquarium should be as near as possible the same temperature as the sea. Bear this in mind when deciding where to put your aquarium. For example, it wouldn't be a good idea to put it on a window sill in direct sunlight. On the other hand, remember that in winter the sea, even near the shore, can be warmer than freshwater ponds or rivers.

Things you might see

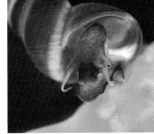

The eye of a gastropod peeping out of its shell (this is a Pink Conch)

The Common Northern Chink Shell on the move with its foot extended

A Cockle with its siphons showing. This means that it is drawing in water to gather oxygen so that it can breathe

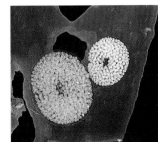

A pair of Slipper-shells mating—see they are connected at the top right

Egg clusters of the Common Northern Chink Shell

Sand & Mud Flats

Although so much of the northern Pacific coast of America is rocky, there are long stretches of sand and mud flats between the many rocky headlands. Sand and mud flats provide homes for many mollusks. They are only uncovered at low tide — don't confuse them with sandy beaches that slope into the water. Collecting can be very good, especially by following trails in the sand, or digging below clam holes.

A snail that lives in these habitats will use its large, single foot to creep across the sand. Many snails browse on fragments of edible material, animal, and vegetable, that are on the surface. Bivalves burrow into the sand or mud, leaving just their feeding siphons projecting. Many of them are filter feeders, drawing in water and filtering out edible particles from it.

Wroblewski's Wentletrap

Like other wentletraps, the snail is white and its shell is grayish white, but sometimes it is stained purple by its own dye. The shell is long, solid, and always looks worn. It has six to eight low, wide, axial ribs. It is fairly common in shallow water from Alaska to southern California.

Wentletrap family
About 1 ins long
First discovered by Moerch in 1876

Beatic Dwarf Olive

Most olive shells are tropical: this is one of the few species that flourishes in cold water. It is a carnivorous scavenger. The shell is long, with a pronounced peak. Its color is a glossy, drab, tan with purplish brown spots. It is moderately common in shallow-water over sand. Its range is from Kodiak Island, Alaska, to Baja California, Mexico.

Olive Shell family
About ½ ins long
First discovered by Carpenter in 1864

Wampum Tusk

As its name implies, this tusk shell was used as wampum (or money) by the Native Americans of the northwest. The shell is moderately curved and solid, an ivory white color, usually with faint yellowish growth rings. It is a common, offshore species living in sandy mud from Alaska to Baja California in Mexico.

Tusk Shell family
About 2 ins long
First discovered by Sowerby in 1860

Gould's Paper-bubble

The shell of this little snail is very fragile. It is globular, translucent yellow in color, with a thin rusty-brown or yellowish orange over-layer. It is a common species, and can be found in intertidal bays, ranging from southern Alaska to the Gulf of California.

Bubble-shell family
About ¾ ins long
First discovered by Gould in 1855

Lewis's Moon Snail

This is a very common, clam-eating species, found in shallow water from British Columbia to southern California. It has a heavy, globular shell, with a small, brown-stained, buttonlike callus at the base.

Moon Snail family – About 4 ins long
First discovered by Gould in 1847

Nuttall's Cockle

Large for a cockle, Nuttall's Cockle has a roundish oval shell, with thirty-three to thirty-seven, coarse, radial ribs. The ribs carry beads shaped like half-moons, but the shells of older cockles are worn smooth. The outside is a drab gray, with a thin, brownish yellow over-layer. This is a common sand-loving cockle, and is found from the Bering Sea and Alaska to southern California.

Cockle family – About 4 ins long
First discovered by Conrad in 1837

Blunt Jackknife Clam

This edible clam is identified by its long, rectangular shell, which is very slightly curved. It is covered with an olive-green, varnishlike over-layer. The clam is common locally on sandy mud flats from British Columbia to California.

Razor Clam family
About 3½ ins long
First discovered by Gould in 1850

Pacific Razor Clam

The shell of this razor clam is an oval-shaped oblong. It is light, but strong. The olive-green over-layer looks like a varnish. The inside of the shell is glossy and white, tinged with purple. This edible clam is very common from Alaska to central California.

Razor Clam family
About 5 ins long
First discovered by Dixon in 1788

Sand & Mud Flats

Hooked Surf Clam

The low beaks of this trough (*say it*: trawff) clam are nearer the rounder rear end. The front end is elongated and narrower. The outside of the shell is chalky, with a shiny brown over-layer. Like other trough shells, an identification pointer is the spoon-shaped recess in the hinge. This clam is common from Washington to California.

Trough Clam family – About 2½ ins long
First discovered by Gould in 1850

Smooth Washington Clam

People in Alaska often eat this venus clam. It has solid, heavy valves, with coarse concentric threads. The valves gape a little at the back end. The color is grayish white. This clam is found from Alaska south to northern California.

Venus Clam family – About 3 ins long
First discovered by Deshayes in 1839

Californian Sunset Clam

This clam belongs to a family similar to the tellins, but larger. The shell is an elongated oval, and the low beaks are nearer the front end. The valves are covered with strong, irregular growth lines. The color is dirty-white with faint purple rays. The over-layer is brown. It is often washed ashore after storms from the Aleutian Islands, Alaska, as far south as California.

Sunset Clam family – About 4 ins long
First discovered by Conrad in 1849

Common Pacific Littleneck

This edible venus clam has a solid shell, sculptured with fine concentric and radial riblets. The color is rusty brown with a purple cast. However, both the color and sculpture can vary. The clam is commonly found in shallow water from the Aleutian Islands, Alaska, to Mexico.

Venus Clam family – About 2 ins long
First discovered by Conrad in 1837

California Soft-shell Clam

Soft-shell clams, also called gapers, are a popular food. This clam is small, with a fragile oval shell. The outside is chalky white, with a gray over-layer. The valves gape very slightly at the rear end. It is common in sand from Alaska to southern California, and then as far south as Peru.

Soft-shell Clam family
About 1¼ ins long
First discovered by
Conrad in 1837

Yoldia-shaped Macoma

The strange name of this tellin comes from Count Yøldi of Sweden, for whom a family of nut clams was named. This tellin has a similar shape to a family known as Yoldia nut clams. It is an elongated oval, white in color, and glossy like porcelain. It is common on sand flats from Alaska to California.

Tellin family
About ½ ins long
First discovered by
Carpenter in 1864

Geoduck

In the Pacific northwest, people call this huge, edible clam the "Gooeyduck." It is commercially fished in Washington and Oregon. The misshapen shell gapes at both ends. The outside of the valves is dirty-white to cream in color, with a thin, yellowish over-layer. The inside is white and semi-glossy. The Geoduck lives in mud at the bottom of a burrow 2–3 feet deep. It is found from Alaska to the Gulf of California.

Saxicave Clam family
About 9 ins long
First discovered by
Conrad in 1849

Great Alaskan Tellin

This tellin's shell is an elongated oval, large, strong and chalky-white, commonly flushed with pink. The over-layer is a greenish brown. It is commonly found at depths of 3–118 feet from Japan to Alaska, and British Columbia.

Tellin family
About 3½ ins long
First discovered by
Wood in 1828

Your Shell Collection

You should concentrate on collecting the shells of dead mollusks. You can study the live animals either on the beach or in an aquarium (see pages 36–7 and 50–1). However, collecting live mollusks is less likely to affect their survival rate than is usually the case. Many mollusks die young because they are eaten or because of changes to their habitat.

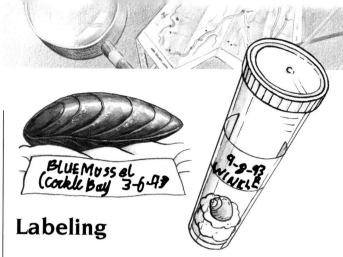

BLUE Mussel
(Cockle Bay 3-6-93

9-9-93
WINKLE

Labeling

When you have cleaned your shells, put them in little Styrofoam trays (the sort that come with vegetables from the supermarket) or plastic boxes, and label each one. Very small shells can be kept in glass or plastic tubes, plugged with cotton.

Your label should give the popular name of the specimen, the scientific name if you know it, when and where you collected it, and any other important or interesting information.

Cleaning

When you take your shells home the first thing to do is to clean them. Most empty shells only need to be rinsed in clean cold water, and perhaps brushed over with an old toothbrush. Be very careful with more fragile shells.

If there is a crust or scale on a shell you can scrape and chip it away, but try not to remove any of the natural coating or weathering of the shell.

If you want to preserve the shell of a live specimen that has died, you will have to remove its soft parts. To do this, put the shell in a saucepan of cold water, bring it to the boil, and then boil it for about 10 minutes. Leave the saucepan to cool naturally, or you may damage the shell.

Or you can put the shell, inside a plastic box, in the microwave oven. Set the oven at high for no more than two minutes for a 600 watt oven, or not more than two and a half minutes in a 500 watt oven. **Always ask permission before you use the stove, saucepans, or microwave oven.**

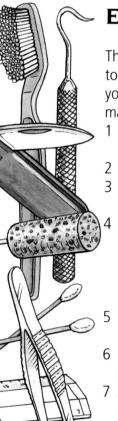

Equipment

This is the equipment you need to manage your collection, plus your field notebook and magnifying glass (see page 36):
1 **An old toothbrush** for cleaning specimens.
2 **A penknife** for cutting.
3 **A dental tool** to scrape away encrustations.
4 **A sharp point** for cleaning small holes. You can make this for yourself by attaching an old darning needle to a wooden handle.
5 **Tweezers** for picking up and holding tiny shells.
6 **Cotton buds** for cleaning out shells.
7 **A short rule**r for checking the size of a shell.
Be careful with all sharp tools.

A home for your collection

It's very easy to make some simple storage units to hold the shells in your collection. They shouldn't cost very much and you can add to them at any time.

All you need are some shoe boxes (with their lids) and some stiff card. If you don't have any shoe boxes at home, visit the local shoe store and ask if you can have some of the ones that customers do not want. Then what you do is this:

1 **Measure the shoe box** across its short side and its depth. Draw a rectangle **(A)** on the card to match this size (eg 6 x 5 ins). Draw two lines across the rectangle to divide it into three.
2 **Measure the long side** (eg 12 x 5 ins.) Draw another rectangle **(B)** to match this size. Draw two lines across it to divide it into three.
3 **Cut out each rectangle**; then cut another one each of **(B)** and **(A)**, using your first rectangles as your patterns. You could have extra partitions.
4 **Pad the bottom of the box** with cotton if you like. Then cut half way up each dividing line of each partition and slot them together as shown. Last, slide the partitions into the box.

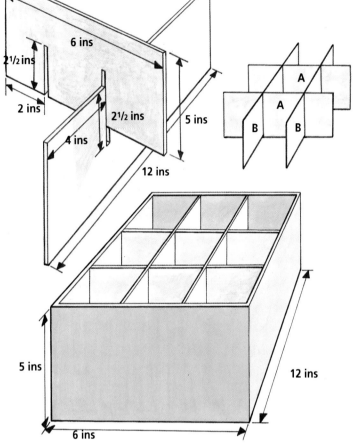

5 **Paint the boxes and their lids** with emulsion paint so that they match. Keep shells of the same family together and write their name on the short end or draw a picture of them there.

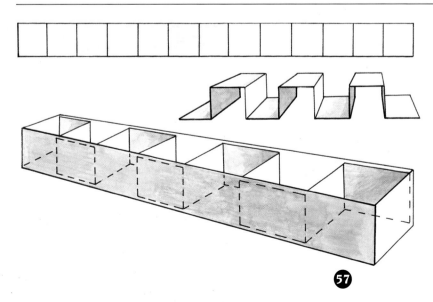

Small scale storage

You can use tin foil or Saranwrap boxes as storage for small shells.

1 **Measure the end of the box** (eg 2 x 2 ins) and draw a strip of these squares on some stiff card.
2 **Cut out the strip** and bend it into a series of right angles as shown.
3 **Fit the bent card into the box** and glue the sides to the box.
4 **Pad the bottom** with cotton if you like and paint them to match.

Pacific Coast: Oregon to California

California extends over more than half the length of the Pacific coast of the United States, excluding Alaska. Rocky coastlines dominate southern Oregon and northern California. The Coast Ranges rise close to the shore, with steep cliffs and narrow beaches, but in between the headlands there are wider, flatter areas, allowing the sand and mud dwelling mollusks to flourish.

Oregon and California as far south as Point Conception are part of what malacologists (shell collectors) call the Oregonian province. Next comes the Californian province, which extends from Point Conception to Baja California in Mexico.

Southern California, from around Santa Barbara southward, has many wide, sandy beaches. The state's rivers provide estuaries where the species of mollusks that are suited to brackish water can breed and flourish.

California's climate is mild, particularly in the south, where it can be very hot in the summer. (Surface sea temperatures range between 52° and 70° Fahrenheit.) This encourages those mollusks that prefer warmer water.

Rocky Shores & Pools

Rocky shores have rough waves, but at low tide you can find mollusks clinging to rocks, or sometimes under hanging seaweeds. There is no better protected area for a group of mollusks and other sea creatures than the pools of clear salt water left behind by the receding tide. The southern Pacific coast is not as rich in rock-dwelling mollusks as the northern Pacific, which is one of the best places in the world to hunt for shells.

All limpets live on rocks. Each limpet's shell grows to fit the patch of rock where it spends its time, so that when it settles down, not even the strongest wave can dislodge it. Often the rim of the shell wears into the rock slightly, giving an even better fit. Limpets may wander around at night or at high tide to graze on algae, but return in the morning to their home patch.

Eroded Periwinkle

The usually badly-worn shell gives this periwinkle its name. The shell is small, with a pointed spire. It is grayish brown with bluish white spots. The aperture is chocolate-brown with a white spiral band at the bottom. The snail is very common on rocky shore flats in the splash zone, from Puget Sound, Washington, to Mexico.

Periwinkle family
About 3/4 ins long
First discovered by Rosewater in 1978

Two-spotted Keyhole Limpet

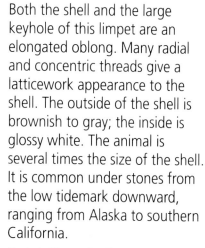

Both the shell and the large keyhole of this limpet are an elongated oblong. Many radial and concentric threads give a latticework appearance to the shell. The outside of the shell is brownish to gray; the inside is glossy white. The animal is several times the size of the shell. It is common under stones from the low tidemark downward, ranging from Alaska to southern California.

Keyhole Limpet family
About 3/4 ins long
First discovered by Dall in 1871

Volcano Limpet

The Volcano Limpet is a typical keyhole limpet, and does look like a miniature volcano. It has a fairly high, oval shell, with an oblong keyhole looking like a tiny crater. There are many large, low radial ribs. The outside is gray, with pinkish mauve radial rays, while the inside is glossy white. In California this limpet is common on rocky rubble in the intertidal zone.

Keyhole Limpet family
About 1 ins long
First discovered by Reeve in 1849

Giant Owl Limpet

This is indeed a giant among limpets, and is commonly found on rocks at the tidemark from California to Mexico. The apex of its massive shell is near the front end. The brown, rough, and sometimes algae-covered shell is glossy inside, with a wide brown border and a bluish central area, sometimes stained brown.

Limpet family – About 4 ins long
First discovered by Sowerby in 1834

Rough Pacific Limpet

The name of this limpet comes from its wavy edge, which is produced by its fifteen to twenty strong, coarse radiating ribs. The shell is a dirty gray-green on the outside, and white with a brown central stain on the inside. It is common from Oregon to Baja California, Mexico. You may find it clinging to gently sloping rock surfaces high above the water line, but within reach of the ocean spray.

American Limpet family
About 1 ins long
First discovered by
Gould in 1846

Scaled Worm Shell

These snails live in colonies attached to rocks or wharves, just below the low water mark. Their home is a shelly tube, which is gray or pinkish. The snail cannot leave the tube, and feeds by trapping particles in the water with thin, sticky, mucus threads. It is common from California as far south as Peru.

Worm Shell family
Tube diameter about ½ ins
First discovered by Carpenter in 1856

Great Keyhole Limpet

This is one of the largest American keyhole limpets. It is found from central California to Baja California, Mexico. Because it is good to eat, it is becoming scarce in Mexico. The animal is black, and its mantle covers most of the shell. The outside of the shell is mauve to brown, covered with fine beads. The keyhole has white edges.

Keyhole Limpet family
Between 3-6 ins long
First discovered by
Sowerby in 1825

Poulson's Dwarf Triton

The shell is solid with a semi-glossy finish. Each whorl has eight or nine lumpy ribs, crossed by many, very fine cut, spiral lines. The grayish or brownish over-layer is thin and smooth. This is a very common species on rocks and wharves, particularly in the southern part of its range, which is from California to Mexico.

Rock Shell family
About 1½ ins long
First discovered by Carpenter in 1864

Checkered Thorn Drupe

The snail's solid shell carries six spiral rows of small, blackish brown squares on a cream background, and has a checkerboard appearance. The outer lip of the aperture also carries brown squares, and there is a small, needle-like spine at its base. The snail is common on rocks above the mid-tidemark from California to Mexico.

Rock Shell family
About ½ ins long
First discovered by Stearns in 1871

Spotted Thorn Drupe

Small, red-brown spots on a bluish gray shell give this snail its name. An all-yellow form is sometimes found. The shell is low-spired, solid, and smoothish except for numerous, faint, spiral threads. The aperture is bluish white. This snail is common at the high tidemark along rocky shores, and among the beds of mussels on which it feeds. It is found from Puget Sound, Washington, to southern California.

Rock Shell family
About 1¼ ins long
First discovered by Blainville in 1832

Livid Macron

The strong, solid shell is yellowish, and covered with a thick, felt-like, dark-brown over-layer. There are five whorls. There are six, cut, spiral lines at the base of the shell. This little whelk is very common and can be found under stones and in rock pools at low tide. Its range is from California south to Mexico.

Buccinum Whelk family
About 1 ins long
First discovered by Adams in 1855

Kellet's Whelk

A very heavy, solid shell is made by this large snail. The bottom of each whorl has ten strong, rounded knobs, and the base of the shell has six to ten cut spiral lines. The aperture is glossy and white. It is very common from northern California to Mexico in rocky areas below the high tidemark. People use baited traps to catch this edible whelk.

Buccinum Whelk family
About 4 ins long
First discovered by Forbes in 1850

Nuttall's Thorn Purpura

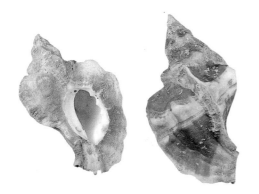

Like other murex and rock shells, this one produces a small quantity of purple dye. It has a solid, heavy, knobby, yellowish brown shell, which is sometimes spirally banded. It has a long, sharp spine on the outer lip (the thorn), which it uses to open barnacles. It is common in the southern part of its range, which is from California to Mexico.

Rock Shell family
About 1½ ins long
First discovered by Conrad in 1837

Clear Jewel Box

This sturdy, spiny bivalve is commonly found attached to wharves, wood pilings and jetties. It is found from Oregon south to Mexico. The white shell is occasionally tinged with pink or olive. It has broad, translucent frills, and the hinge has a large irregular tooth.

Jewel Box family
About 3 ins long
First discovered by Bernard in 1976

Sand & Mud Flats

Sand and mud flats provide homes for many mollusks. They are only uncovered at low tide — don't confuse them with sandy beaches that slope into the water. Collecting can be very good, especially by following trails in the sand, or digging below clam holes. Although so much of the northern Pacific coast of America is rocky, there are extensive stretches of sand and mud flats between the many rocky headlands.

A snail that lives in these habitats will use its large, single foot to creep across the sand. Many snails browse on fragments of edible material, animal, and vegetable, that are on the surface. Bivalves burrow into the sand or mud, leaving just their feeding siphons projecting. Many of them are filter feeders, drawing in water and filtering out edible particles from it.

Giant Western Nassa

Although not big, this is one of the largest known nassa snails. It feeds on dead animal matter. The shell is orange-brown to gray; the last whorl has about twelve coarse spiral threads crossed by short axial riblets. It is common in intertidal zones from Vancouver Island, British Columbia, to Mexico.

Nassa Mud Snail family
About 1½ ins long
First discovered by Gould in 1849

Oldroyd's Fragile Moon Snail

A thin, globular shell, a little wider than high, distinguishes this snail. There is an umbilical hole in the base of the shell. It lives in large colonies offshore, in sandy areas from Oregon to southern California. There it feeds on small bivalves and lays its eggs in sandy collars.

Moon Snail family
About 2½ ins long
First discovered by Dall in 1897

Sowerby's Paper-bubble

A very large, open aperture and a fragile shell are characteristics of this little snail. The translucent, globular shell is greenish yellow in color. The animal is dark green with yellowish markings. This snail is a common, shallow-water species of the open coast. It prefers sandy areas where there are beds of sea grass. There it lays its egg masses on weed stems. It is found from Puget Sound, Washington, south to the Gulf of California.

Bubble Shell family
About ½ ins long
First discovered by Sowerby in 1833

Purple Dwarf Olive

Shaped like a tubby football, the Purple Dwarf Olive has a solid, glossy shell. The color is a bluish gray, and there are violet stains around the lower part of the aperture. During the summer months, this snail is very common in sandy bays and beaches, from Vancouver Island, British Columbia, south to Baja California in Mexico.

Olive Shell family
About 1 ins long
First discovered by Sowerby in 1825

Carinate Dove-shell

The shoulder of the last whorl of this tiny shell is swollen, forming the "carina" (or keel-like ridge) which gives it its name. The shell is smooth and glossy; its color is a mixture of orange, white, and brown. This is a common, shallow-water species, which is found on weeds in sandy areas from California to Mexico.

Dove-shell family
About ¼ ins long
First discovered by Hinds in 1844

Western Fat Nassa

Neat, beaded sculpturing characterizes this nassa mud snail. The shell is thin, but strong, with a straight, pointed spire. The aperture is less than half the length of the shell. Most of the the shell is a yellowish brown. It is extremely common on intertidal flats off Vancouver Island, British Columbia, south to Baja California, Mexico.

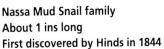

Nassa Mud Snail family
About 1 ins long
First discovered by Hinds in 1844

Sand & Mud Flats

Californian Mactra

This is a small clam, fairly common in Californian lagoons. It has a smooth, not very strong, elongated, oval shell. There are concentric undulations on the beaks. The over-layer is a velvety yellowish brown. There is a small, spoon-shaped hollow in the center of the hinge.

Mactra Surf Clam family
About 2 ins long
First discovered by Conrad in 1837

Senhouse's Mussel

This small mussel was introduced from Asia, and now flourishes from Washington to central California. It makes its nest on mud flats and clings to wooden pilings. The shell is small, thin, and fragile. It is smooth and green to bluish green in color with delicate, zigzag, brownish marks.

Mussel family
About 1 ins long
First discovered by
Benson in 1842

Modest Tellin

Common in sandy areas from Alaska to Mexico, the Modest Tellin is a small, thin-shelled bivalve. The shell is long and compressed laterally. It has fine concentric grooves, and is white with an iridescent sheen. The two hinge teeth are very small.

Tellin family
About 3/4 ins long
First discovered by
Carpenter in 1864

Northern Horse Mussel

This is one of the most common mussels found in northern waters, living in huge colonies below the high tidemark, as far south as central California on the Pacific coast, and New Jersey on the Atlantic coast. It has a strong, oblong, swollen shell. Adult shells are chalky mauve-white in color, covered by a thick, blackish brown over-layer.

Mussel family – About 4 ins long
First discovered by
Linnaeus in 1758

Salmon Tellin

Smaller than the Modest Tellin, the Salmon Tellin has a white oval shell, with several widely spaced growth lines, stained dark brown. The inside of the shell is tinted rose. It is common from the low tidemark downward, from the Aleutian Islands, Alaska, to central California.

Tellin family
About ½ ins long
First discovered by Reeve in 1845

Californian Mussel

This mussel has a large, thick shell. The ventral margin, opposite the hinge, is curved. The outer surface has coarse growth lines and twelve, weak, radial ribs. It is very common in the intertidal zone from the Aleutian Islands, Alaska, to Mexico.

Mussel family
About 5 ins long
First discovered by Conrad in 1837

Alaskan Gaper

The Alaskan Gaper is a very large clam, an elongated-oval in shape. It gapes open at the rear end. It lives in sandy mud in shallow water, from Alaska to northern California, and is common.

Mactra Surf Clam family
About 8 ins long
First discovered by Gould in 1850

Sand & Mud Flats

Bent-nosed Macoma

The rear end of the shell is compressed and strongly twisted to the right—hence its common name. The shell is sturdy and chalky-white. The left valve is nearly flat. There are two tiny teeth at the center of the narrow hinge. It is a very common species, living in mud in quiet waters, and is found from southern Alaska to Mexico.

Tellin family
About 3 ins long
First discovered by Conrad in 1837

White Sand Macoma

This fairly large, white bivalve lives in sand in bays and intertidal flats, and is common from British Columbia to Mexico. The shell is large, with an almost flat left valve and an inflated right valve. There is a large, rib-like ridge behind the hinge inside each valve.

Tellin family – About 3½ ins long
First discovered by Conrad in 1837

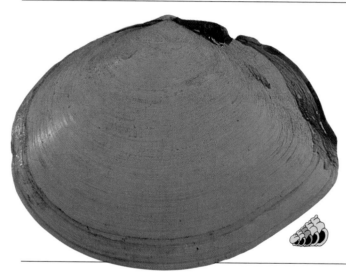

Common Washington Clam

Despite its name, this clam is only found between northern California and Baja California, Mexico. It is a very common, edible species, living in shallow water. The shell is solid and oblong. The outside is covered with coarse, crowded, concentric riblets. The color is a dull reddish brown, varying to gray with rust stains. The inside is a glossy white, with touches of purple. It is also called the Butter Clam.

Venus Clam family
About 3½ ins long
First discovered by Conrad in 1837

California Lyonsia

The small, elongated shell of this clam is very fragile, and is almost transparent. The outside is opalescent white, and is commonly covered with the weak, dark, radial lines of the over-layer. It is common in sandy mud bottoms in many California marshy inlets and bays.

Lyonsia Clam family
About 1 ins long
First discovered by Conrad in 1837

Filipino Venus

This clam was introduced, probably accidentally, from eastern Asia, and now flourishes in the waters of Puget Sound, Washington, and off California. Its shell is almost egg-shaped, and the beaks are nearer the front end. The outside has radial threads and is beaded at the hind end. The inside of the shell is tinged with purple. This mollusk is also known as the Japanese Littleneck.

Venus Clam family
About 2 ins long
First discovered by Adams and Reeve in 1850

Pismo Clam

From California to Mexico this edible clam is a common shore species. It has a large, heavy shell, which is glossy and smooth, except for weak growth-line, and brownish cream with wide, mauve radial rays. The over-layer is thin and glossy.

Venus Clam family
About 3 ins long
First discovered by Maive in 1823

Punctate Pandora

The Punctate Pandora is a very common, small, flat, cold-water clam, which lives in sandy mud from the low tidemark downward. The shell is crescent-shaped. It is found from Vancouver Island, British Columbia, to Baja California, Mexico.

Pandora Clam family
About 1 ins long
First discovered by Conrad in 1837

Estuaries & Marshes

The waters of river estuaries are brackish, a mixture of salt water from the sea and fresh water from the river. Brackish water is also found in lagoons. These are shallow bodies of water close to the sea. Only certain species of mussels and clams do well in brackish water, although oysters also enjoy this habitat. Wading birds, ducks, horseshoe crabs, and blue crabs feed on estuary mollusks.

Californian Bubble

The shell is large for a bubble, and the animal is bigger than the shell. The aperture extends the full length of the shell, which is a grayish brown with darker brown streaks. The snail is most active at night, but also look for it on mud flats at low tide.

Bubble Shell family
About 1½ ins long
First discovered by Pilsbry in 1895

Common Californian Venus

This sturdy shell has many low, radial ribs, crossed by raised concentric ribs, giving it a checkerboard appearance. The inside of the shell is white with a purple blotch at one end. It is found from southern California to Panama. This edible clam lives in sand from the intertidal zone downward.

Venus Clam family
About 2 ins long
First discovered by Broderip in 1835

Pacific Littleneck

This clam is valued as a food, and fortunately it is very common in the intertidal zone. It is found from Alaska to Baja California. The shell has many radial and concentric ribs. In southern California the clams are beaded and crisscrossed. The color varies from white to chocolate brown; sometimes the shell has a mottled pattern.

Venus Clam family – About 2 ins long
First discovered by Conrad in 1837

Californian Donax

This wedge clam has a thin shell, longer and slightly larger than that of its relative, Gould's Donax. The outside is yellowish white, with a tan or greenish over-layer. Inside it is whitish with a purple blotch at each end of the hinge. It is common in the intertidal zone from California to Baja California, Mexico. Look for it in coves and bays.

Wedge Clam family
About 1 ins long
First discovered by Conrad in 1837

Norris Top Shell

This top-shell lives among kelp, eating food particles clinging to the seaweed. It is common from Monterey, California, to Baja California, Mexico. The shell is smooth, heavy and solid. It is a glossy, blackish brown. The operculum is circular and has rows of dense bristles.

Top-shell family
About 1½ ins long
First discovered by Sowerby in 1838

Common Northern Lacuna

This tiny lacuna periwinkle is a cold-water species, and is common offshore in shallow water on kelp. It is found from Alaska to California on the Pacific coast, and from Labrador south to Rhode Island on the Atlantic coast. It has a fairly thin, but strong, translucent shell. There is a small chink, or slit, in the bottom of the shell. The outside is smooth except for microscopic spiral scratches. The color varies from light tan to brown, with the spire tinted a purplish rose.

Lacuna Periwinkle family
About ¼ ins long
First discovered by Montagu in 1803

Non-boring Date Mussel

This little mussel has a shape that might be regarded as typical of the family, elongated and slightly curved. Its negative-sounding name is to distinguish from most other date mussels, which bore into rock. The shell is chestnut-brown. It is a very common species, living in colonies attached to wharves, pilings, and jetties. It is found from Oregon south to Mexico.

Mussel family
About 1 ins long
First discovered by Dall in 1911

False Pacific Jingle

The shell is fairly strong, almost circular, with very coarse, irregular radiating ribs. The lower valve has a hole. The color is greenish white, and inclined to be pearly. It is commonly found on stones, wharves, and pilings, but it is also often found on other shells, particularly abalone shells. It lives all around the Pacific from Japan through Alaska to Mexico.

Jingle Shell family – About 3 ins long
First discovered by Deshayes in 1839

Things To Make

Shells make excellent decorations. Some of the large tropical shells are ornaments on their own, but many small shells can be used to decorate other objects.

Decorate with shells

The best way to attach the shells is to put a layer of modeling clay or ready-mixed wall filler over the object you wish to decorate—a box, vase, or bottle. Press the shells into the clay to make a pattern, using shells of different sizes and colors. After the clay dries out, you can coat the whole with varnish to protect it and give it a glossy finish.

Wreath of shells

This is a good way of displaying your shells and also makes an unusual present.

1 **Take a generous handful of straw** and twist it into a "snake."
2 **Wind twin wire tightly round** the straw to hold it together and make it tight and firm.
3 **Bring the two ends of your snake together** and overlap them. It will help if the ends are thinner than the rest of the snake. The wire will then bind the snake into a ring.
4 **You can attach the shells** to the ring with wire or pins, but it is better to stick them on with a quick-drying PVA glue.

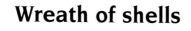

Jewelry from the sea

Small shells make beautiful and unusual jewelry. Why not make yourself a pendant or a brooch?

1. **Buy a bell cap and ring** from your local craft or hobby store and some PVA glue.
2. **Choose a fine example of a shell** and wash it carefully in warm soapy water and leave it to dry.

3. **Glue the bell mount to the top** of your shell and leave it to dry.
4. **Thread the ring through** the bell mount and pinch the ring tight (you may need help for this). Thread the pendant on to a ribbon or chain.

5. **For a brooch,** glue the mount to the side of the shell next to the opening as shown.
6. **To make the shells shine,** you can paint a coat of varnish over them.

Birds and monsters

Use two different gastropod shells, glued together, to make a series of exotic birds. Add a small feather to form the tail and make them more lifelike.

You can also invent your own creatures by sticking together shells to make monsters. Don't stick more than two shells together at a time and let them dry before adding more. Here are some ideas to start you off.

Atlantic Coast Borers

The borers are a group of bivalves which bore holes. Some tunnel into wood, and may eat some of it. Others tunnel into rock for shelter. The boring is done by the front edge of the shell, which is rocked to and fro to wear away the wood or rock tunnel.

Borers are all bivalves, but they come from a diverse range of families. Most of them bore to make a home where they can shelter from predators. The sharp edges of their valves are the cutting tools they use. The species shown on page 75 are all from the Atlantic coast, while the ones on pages 76–77 are from the Pacific coast.

Gould's Shipworm

The so-called shipworms are not worms at all, though they have long bodies like earthworms. They are bivalves, but with very small shells, which do not enclose more than a fraction of the animals' bodies. In the days of wooden ships they were a very real menace to shipping. As the picture shows, the damage caused by shipworms is immense.

Living animals are common in floating logs, wharves, pilings, and other underwater timbers. As it grows a shipworm burrows into the wood, leaving behind it a long, shell-lined tunnel connected to the open sea. The animal grips the inside of the tunnel with its foot, and twists its valves back and forth to wear away the timber. It absorbs food from the sea water, which it takes in through a siphon which protrudes from the hole. It can also digest some of the cellulose from the timber. In all species, the siphons can be withdrawn, and the hole is then closed by a pair of feathery, limy plates that are called "pallets."

There are several dozen species of shipworms; their identification is difficult, and can only be made with live specimens—Gould's Shipworm is a typical example.

Shipworm family
About 8 ins long
First discovered by Bartsch in 1908

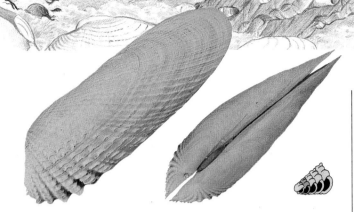

False Angel Wing

You can see from the angle of the picture why this shell is called the False Angel Wing. If you see a live specimen, you will see it has a large, translucent, gray siphon. It bores holes into peat and clay, and is common from the Gulf of St Lawrence to Texas. It has a long, fragile, chalky-white shell.

Rock-borer family – About 2 ins long
First discovered by Linnaeus in 1818

Striate Martesia

This little piddock is usually pear-shaped, although the shape does vary. The foot-gape between the two valves is wide. The shell is white, with a tan over-layer. Fine, concentric, parallel threads cover the outside. This piddock is common in floating or submerged wood from North Carolina to Texas and beyond. You will have to dig it out with a sharp tool.

Piddock family
About 1 ins long
First discovered by Linnaeus in 1758

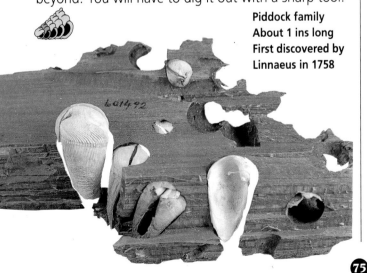

Angel Wing

The two valves of this huge clam could easily be the models for an angel's wings. The long, thin shell is pure white with a thin gray over-layer. Each valve has about thirty beaded axial ribs. It is common in shallow water where it burrows almost 12 inches deep in the mud. It is common in the southeastern United States in quiet waters.

Piddock family – About 6 ins long
First discovered by Linnaeus in 1758

Smith's Martesia

This tiny bivalve also belongs to the family of wood- and mud-boring clams known as piddocks. It is small, oblong, and wedge-shaped, and has a white shell. It tunnels into soft rocks or, as here, into the shells of oysters. It is common from Massachusetts south to Texas.

Piddock family
About ¼ ins long
First discovered by Tryon in 1862

Pacific Coast Borers

The Pacific coast has a number of piddocks that bore into clay or sand for shelter. Unfortunately it also has the destructive shipworms (see page 74).

Falcate Date Mussel

This is a fairly common rock-borer in shallow water from Coos Bay, Oregon, to Mexico. It has a very elongated, cylindrical shell, which is slightly curved. The beaks of the valves are about one-eighth the length from the swollen front end. The color is a shiny chestnut-brown.

Mussel family
About 3 ins long
First discovered by Gould in 1851

Californian Date Mussel

This is similar to the Falcate Date Mussel, but chubbier and much smaller. It has a smooth surface, and is chocolate-brown in color. A velvety, hairy over-layer covers the rear end. The mussel makes burrows in hard rocks in shallow water. It is moderately common from British Columbia to southern California.

Mussel family
About 1 ins long
First discovered by Philippe in 1847

Fan-shaped Horse Mussel

This large mussel lives buried in mud. It has a rectangular shell, slightly curved, and is not really very fan-shaped, despite its name. Thin growth lines cover the outside, which is bluish white with a yellowish brown over-layer. The inside is pearly white, tinged with pink. Its range is from British Columbia to Mexico.

Mussel family
About 5 ins long
First discovered by Conrad in 1837

Gabb's Piddock

This borer tunnels into sandstone rocks and clay from Drier Bay, Alaska, to San Pedro, California. It is fairly common. The siphons are fused together and pimply. The shell is thin, but strong, with an oblique groove across the outside. It is white in color with yellowish marks.

Piddock family – About 2 ins long
First discovered by George Tryon in 1863

Boring Soft-shell Clam

Living in holes bored in hard-packed clay or soft sandstone does not save this edible clam from people who want to eat it. It has a solid, oblong shell, covered with concentric lines that look like clapboard. The outside is chalky white, with a thin over-layer that is brownish or rusty. It is found from British Columbia to southern California.

Soft-shell Clam family – About 2½ ins long
First discovered by Conrad in 1837

Flat-tipped Piddock

This is the most common piddock to be found along the Pacific coast. It bores into stiff, blue clay, sandstone and cement, and you can find it from Alaska all the way down to Mexico. Its siphons are smooth. The plates are an elongated oval.

Piddock family – About 3½ ins long
First discovered by Conrad in 1837

Wart-necked Piddock

You will find the burrow of this large piddock in soft shale rock below the low tidemark. It has a fat, oblong shell, divided by an oblique groove in the middle of each valve. It also has very large, warty siphons, which give this piddock its popular name. It is found from California to Mexico.

Piddock family – About 3 ins long
First discovered by Gould in 1851

Find Out Some More

Useful Organizations

There are over seventy-five shell clubs located in major cities throughout the United States and Canada. All welcome new members. They are all listed in the membership bulletins of the three leading national shell societies (see below). Check with the nearest natural history museum, your school librarian or the local public library for information on them.

The **American Malacological Union** is an organization of professionals and hobbyists, and publishes the *American Malacological Bulletin*. Write to: American Malacological Union, P.O. Box 30, North Myrtle Beach, SC 29582.

The **Conchologists of America** is a collector-oriented society, promoting shellfish conservation and environmentally-sound collecting practices. It publishes quarterly *American Conchologist*. Write to: Conchologists of America, c/o Lynn Scheu, 1222 Holsworth Lane, Louisville, KY 40222.

For Pacific Coast enthusiasts there is the **Western Society of Malacologists**, open to professionals and amateurs. Write to: Western Society of Malacologists, c/o Dr. Henry Chaney, 1633 Posilipo Lane, Santa Barbara, CA 93108.

For a complete listing of **National Wildlife Refuges**, which include many seaside areas, write to: Division of National Wildlife Refuges, Fish and Wildlife Department, Room 2343, Washington DC 20240.

There is no national shell club for **Canada**. The US societies listed here cover Canada as well.

Places To Visit

You can look for shells and mollusks on almost any beach, but some locations naturally produce better, or more varied, specimens than others.

Along the **East Coast**, the best shelling is on sand beaches. Cape Cod, Massachusetts, forms a natural boundary—the most southerly point for many cold-water species, and the most northerly point for many southern shells.

Farther south, the beaches of Assateague Island National Seashore (including Chincoteague National Wildlife Refuge) in Maryland and Virginia are excellent for shell-collecting, as are the beaches of the Outer Banks in North Carolina.

Florida is one of the best shell-collecting regions in North America, with its gentle sand beaches and diverse selection of subtropical species; in fact, almost any beach will do. However, Sanibel and Captiva Islands on the Gulf Coast are justly famous for the quality of their shelling. Sanibel also has a Shell Museum, displaying many unusual specimens.

On the **West Coast**, state and national parks and public seashores offer the easiest access for collectors. The coastal units of the Olympic National Park in Washington state offer shelling for scallops and other mollusks, as well as the park's famous tide pools, where live shellfish can be found.

In Oregon, Yaquina Head Natural Area on the northern coast features both smooth beaches and tide pools.

Hidden Beach and other coastal areas in Redwood National Park in northern California are overshadowed by the big trees, but are worth a visit by collectors.

Index & Glossary

To find the name of a mollusk, search under its main name. So, to look up Atlantic Surf Clam, look under Clam, not under Surf.

A

Amphissa, Joseph's Coat, 47

Angel Wing, False, 75

aperture: main opening of a gastropod shell 13

apex: the point of the *spire* of a gastropod shell 10

Ark, Blood, 31

Ark, Ponderous, 31

Ark, Transverse, 29

Ark, Zebra, 28

Auger, Atlantic, 35

B

Baby's Ear, Common, 30

beak: first bit of a bivalve's shells to form, just above the *hinge* 34, 43, 58

Bonnet, Scotch, 33

Bubble, Californian, 70

Bubble, West Indian, 40

byssus thread: a sort of rope used by molluscs to anchor themselves to rocks 8, 34, 36

C

canal: the channel at the lower end of a gastropod shell through which the *siphons* are extended 16

Cardita, Broad-ribbed, 34

Chiton, Lined Red, 49

Chiton, Merten's, 49

Chiton, Northern Red, 49

Cingula, Pointed, 18

Clam, Amethyst Gem, 20

Clam, Atlantic Jackknife, 16

Clam, Atlantic Nut, 14

Clam, Atlantic Razor, 16

Clam, Atlantic Surf, 15

Clam, Blunt Jackknife, 53

Clam, Boring Soft-shell, 77

Clam, Calfornia Soft-shell, 55

Clam, Calico, 35

Clam, Californian Sunset, 54

Clam, Carolina Marsh, 41

Clam, Common Washington, 68

Clam, Hooked Surf, 54

Clam, Pacific Razor, 53

Clam, Pismo, 69

Clam, Pointed Nut, 39

Clam, Smooth Washington, 54

Clam, Soft-shell, 17

Cockle, Morton's Egg, 39

Cockle, Nuttall's, 53

Cockle, Prickly, 34

Conch, Florida Fighting, 32

Cone, Florida, 34

contrary: any gastropod shell coiling to the left 52

Coquina, 17

cords, spiral: horizontal bands on a whorl 7, 17

D

Dogwinkle, Atlantic, 10

Dogwinkle, Emarginate, 48

Dogwinkle, File, 48

Dogwinkle, Frilled, 48

Donax, Californian, 70

Dove-shell, Carinate, 65

Dove-shell, Common, 34

Dove-shell, Lunar, 38

Drill, Atlantic Oyster, 19

Drill, Thick-lipped, 18

Drupe, Checkered Thorn, 62

Drupe, Spotted Thorn, 62

E

ears: like handles, found on scallop shells by the point from which the ribs radiate 62, 63

F

Fig Shell, Common, 32

G

gape: the opening between the two *valves* which remains when a bivalve is closed 34, 35, 67

Gaper, Alaskan, 67

Geoduck, 55

H

hinge: the pivoting point from which a bivalve opens and closes 19

Useful Books

The Edge of the Sea, Rachel Carson (Houghton Mifflin Co., 1955) A classic of nature writing that explores the life of the coast.

Peterson First Guide to Shells and Seashores, (Houghton Milflin Co., 1992) For beginners, illustrates the most common species of shells.

Field Guide to Shells of the Atlantic and Gulf Coasts and *Field Guide to Shells of the Pacific Coast and Hawaii,* Percy Morris (Peterson, Houghton Mifflin Co.) For more experienced collectors.

Seashells of North America, R. Tucker Abbott (Golden Press, 1986) A popular pocket guide.

Collectible Florida Shells, R. Tucker Abbott (American Malacologists, 1992). Good guide to finding and collecting Florida's spectacular shells.

Seashells of the Northern Hemisphere, R. Tucker Abbott (Smithmark, 1991). Covers coldwater species from the northern Atlantic & Pacific.

Index & Glossary

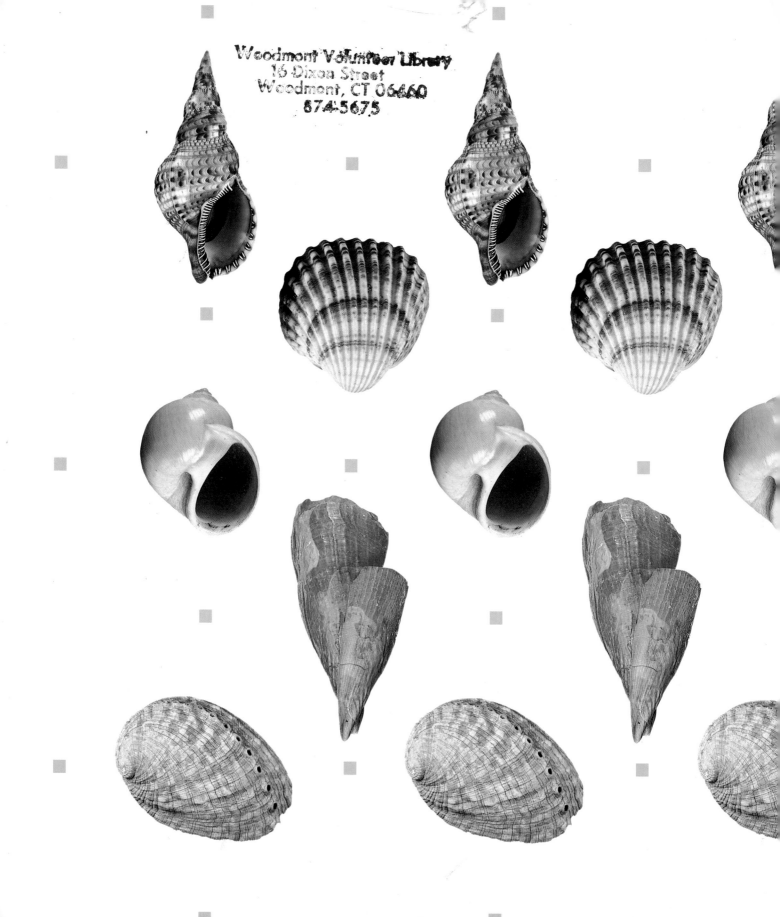